Anonymous

Portsmouth Monumental Cook Book

Anonymous

Portsmouth Monumental Cook Book

ISBN/EAN: 9783744788854

Printed in Europe, USA, Canada, Australia, Japan

Cover: Foto ©Andreas Hilbeck / pixelio.de

More available books at **www.hansebooks.com**

PORTSMOUTH MONUMENTAL COOK BOOK,

COMPILED BY THE

LADIES OF THE SOLDIERS' AID SOCIETY,

OF

PORTSMOUTH, OHIO.

"It is good to learn from the experience of others."

PORTSMOUTH:
JAS. W. NEWMAN, PRINTER, TIMES OFFICE.
1874.

Entered according to the Act of Congress, in the year 1874, by the Ladies of the Soldiers' Aid Society, of Portsmouth, Ohio, in the office of the Librarian of Congress, at Washington.

PREFACE.

I do not propose to enter into any disquisition on the art *cuisine*, though "what I know" about it might not be less than would prevent one from making such use of the materials of which food is composed, to keep one from starving.

Those for the perpetuation of whose memory this book is compiled, suffered little on the tented or untented field for lack of knowledge of the art of cooking. They could prepare meals that their General could most generally relish, for Generals had appetites as well those who were "only privates." Whatever else was wanting, they were rarely without that most excellent condiment that seldom fails to make even ordinary food palatable; yet, good as it is, it is seldom in demand, never advertised or offered for sale, and when possessed, the possessor wants to get rid of it; and compared to which, all other sauce would be but a saucy fraud. The sauce to which I refer has the significant cognomen of Hunger Sauce. For further particulars, inquire within after having fasted—say, twenty-four hours. If you want to fasten what I mean on your minds, and know any faster way to do it, I shall still be your fast friend. If you would wait for a weightier definition, then dismiss the desire for the present, and if the opportunity to go to war should present itself, and your thirst for this special knowledge remains unsatiated, and you are hungry for a fight, you have only to enlist, draw your rations with the regularity and unstinted variety (vegetable and animal food in lively combination, is here meant) for which rations are noted, and you will not be long in attaining to a rational idea of what I am trying so hard to explain. Your hunger for fight will probably not survive your first skirmish, and possibly not your first night in camp, and therefore may not be longer dwelt upon. A change of residence becomes desirable when the atmosphere becomes heavy on account of a surcharge of particles of lead and iron, together with the unpleasant smell of sulphur, and though such residence has been of long standing, it is just as apt to end in right down lying. And then should your mess pronounce your first mess of beans and pork an unpalatable mess, they will lay less stress on the shortcomings of the second. While you improve they will appreciate, and cease to complain for conscience sake.

Rotation in the office of cook begets a fellow feeling that makes us wondrous kind. Speaking of conscience, I am reminded that I have known it to lose its sensitiveness to some extent when a smoke-house was scented near the line of march. It made little difference whether it was March or September, or "forward march," a march was stolen on that smoke-house, and all of Bacon's moral precepts would not have saved that bacon, or brought a single tingle to the conscience. True, not every one would have taken that bacon, but all would have eaten it. Even the chaplain was not averse to a transverse section of the middle of a fine ham.

So much for what I am not going to do.

What I would gladly do, would be to pay a tribute to the noble women who, having given up those who were dearest to them, and having bidden them go forth bearing their shields, and admonishing them, as did the women of Sparta, to return bearing them or being borne on them, immediately organized into societies for the purpose of rendering such aid as would most speedily conduce to the accomplishment of the end sought, and as by one common impulse those societies, which numbered thousands, were bound together by a sentiment which arose to a high and holy enthusiasm, evincing a patriotism than which the world has known none deeper, higher, broader, nor more firmly grounded in the heart's best promptings.

Actuated by a clear conviction that the cause they espoused was just, they, no less than the soldiers in the field, laid their lives on the altar of their country, and believing the cause was also God's cause, invoked His blessing on the consecration they would make, and believing that He would lead, however difficult the way, never hesitated to plunge into duty, however dark the adversity that loomed up against them. I would gladly portray so vividly the soul-earnestness, the abandonment of every selfish thought and purpose for the good of the boys in blue, that even now, at this distant day, the women so engaged might be held in yet higher honor for the deeds they wrought, and for the far-reaching results of those deeds. Were my pen a pen of fire, and had it the speed of the lightning, and had I for a parchment the blackness of midnight spread out all over the canopy of heaven, and had I the language of angels, I yet could not sufficiently portray the grandeur of the work performed, or indicate to what extent victory hung upon those deeds. The war was prolific of wounds, sickness and death; but amid all, these women ever kept pace with the rapid evolution of events, staying not for heat, or cold, or pestilence, or danger in any of its forms, and rarely failed to demonstrate that they were masters of the situation. Where there was a brow burning with fever; where there was a wound to be bound up; wherever there was a soul to be lured back from the grave; where there was a heart grown faint because its loved ones were not, and wherever mercy called, though but faintly, and woman could reach the spot, she was there, and to falter till the work was *done*, is not told in the annals, written or unwritten, of what women did in the war. Many of those who thus labored fell in the midst of their labors; others soon followed after the work was done; and others still live, upon whose heads the light of eternity is glinting in rays of silver, yet young in the thought that God permitted them to live and to labor in so great a cause, and to do and be spent in a reform so grand. They live and labor yet, deeming their work incomplete until they shall have erected monuments to those who fell, and also to those who are yet spared to enjoy the blessings secured by their toiling and their courageous daring, and before whom is yet death's open door. Then to all who yet remember what those four dark years meant, when war hovered as a pall over the nation, and that the daring of our men and the exalted patriotism of our women saved it, I would say, extend them your help in this their crowning work, and it can not be long until their labor of love will be complete; and the monument they shall have raised to the honored dead shall also stand for a monument to the nobility of woman, but can not honor her more than that set up in the soldier's heart, which is, and shall be, more enduring than granite.

I speak from the standpoint of one who knows whereof he affirms in all that pertains to woman's self imposed toiling during that dark period. Her heroism was none the less marked because she may never have seen a battle, for it required more than heroism to take upon herself the constant burden of care for the sick and the maimed; that burden even sharing her pillow when she sought that rest that would enable her to take it up anew. Yet all this was her joy, her meat, her drink, could she minister with her hand and heart to the wants of one dying man. Now that the storm-cloud has receded far into the distance, and white-winged peace hovers smiling over all the land, and the record of the past wears a halo that only the recollection of duty done could impart, that the highest success may attend this final and crowning enterprise, is the wish of one whose debt of gratitude is such that he can not hope to repay or wish to forget it.

INDEX TO ADVERTISEMENTS.

BANKS.
	PAGE.
First National	153
Farmers' National	165

BAKERS AND CONFECTIONERS.
Albert Knittel	156
A. Seel	170

BOOTS, SHOES, AND HATS.
WHOLESALE.
C. P. Tracy & Co	158
Hibbs, Richardson & Co	159

RETAIL.
J. W. March & Co	174
R. M. Lloyd	178

BOOKS AND STATIONERY.
Geo. W. Watkins	164
Valley Book Store	169

BAKING POWDERS.
A. D. Miller	172

CLOTHING.
Miller, Voorheis & Co	158
Lehman, Richman & Co	171

CONFECTIONERS.
V. Reinhart & Co	163
B. Augustin	173

COAL DEALERS.
	PAGE.
W. W. Little & Co	165

CARRIAGE MAKER.
John Dice	176

DENTIST.
C. P. Dennis	167

DRUGGISTS.
D. R. Spry	159
Davis & Jones	169
Enos Reed	172
H. P. Pursell	164
George Fisher	166
M. S. Pixley	178

DRY GOODS.
WHOLESALE.
Jas. M. Rumsey & Co	154
J. F. Towell	162

RETAIL.
P. Brodbeck	156
W. A. Connolley	157
J. N. Leedom	158
R. Brunner	161
W. H. Johnson & Co	168

FIRE BRICK WORKS.
Scioto Star Fire Brick Co	171
Scioto Valley Fire Brick Co	176

INDEX TO ADVERTISEMENTS.

FRUITS, GAME AND TOYS
PAGE.
W. E. Hancock 175

FURNITURE.
J. H. Wait & Son 155
J. B. Nichols & Co 155
Cabinet Makers' Union 155

FLOUR AND GRAIN.
M. W. Thompson & Son 171
Geo. Davis & Co 177

GROCERIES.
WHOLESALE.
Damarin & Co 163
RETAIL.
H. H. Buskirk 163
W. I. Gray & Co 166
Fisher & Co 167
John Wilhelm 167
M. F. Micklethwait & Bro 175
M. & S. Timmonds 177

GASFITTING AND PLUMBING.
John Jones 167

HATS AND CAPS.
Scioto Hat Co 175

HARDWARE.
Hibbs, Angle & Co 156
J. L. Hibbs & Co 159

HOTELS.
Biggs House 161
Massie House 161
St. James Hotel 179
Crawford House 180
Walnut Street House 179

INSURANCE.
W. H. Bonsall & Co 173

JEWELER.
Ph. Zellner 157

LIVERY STABLES.
PAGE.
T. M. Lynn 164
Yeager & Dice 170

LUMBER DEALERS.
H. Leet & Co 177

MARBLE DEALER.
Ch. C. Bode 174

MERCHANT TAILORS.
E. Miller 154
A. Lorberg 176
L. R. Morgan 172

MILLINERY.
Mrs. Nickells & Co 163
Miss M. Lloyd 165
Misses Coe & Keer 165
Mrs. Trotter 166

MUSICAL INSTRUMENTS.
John Yoakley 173
D. S. Johnston 173

NOTIONS AND WHITE GOODS.
Reed & Peebles 170

NOTIONS AND STAMPING.
Miss E. Bell 174

QUEENSWARE AND CHINA.
Pursell, Ewing & Co 160

STOVE DEALERS.
H. Eberhardt & Co 175

SEWING MACHINES.
J. T. Grayson 152
Geo. D. Selby 153

STONE DEALERS.
Reitz & Bode 174

TINNERS.
Wilhelm & Conroy 167

SOUP.

GENERAL DIRECTIONS.

Soup should not be distinguished by any flavor, all ingredients being so blended that none seem prominent. A tin vessel is considered best; never use brass or copper. Iron may be used, if kept clean and fresh. A camp kettle is considered good, having a heavy lid, it retains the steam.

Never let soup stand to get cold in the vessel in which it is cooked. Pour it immediately into the tureen.

Always put the meat in cold water, thus the juices are extracted.

Meat should be lean and fresh.

Soft water is best. One quart of water to one pound of meat, is a common rule; if the soup is desired richer, use less water.

Let the meat boil very slow at first; it is best to merely simmer, thus the impurities will rise to the top and may be skimmed off. The common flavorings are catsup, spices, celery, mushrooms, onions, herbs, etc. It is best to be careful of seasoning of all kinds, particularly salt and pepper, as too little can be remedied; too much cannot.

A wooden spoon is best for stirring soup.

Mrs. Hale, in her new book on cookery, gives the following soup powders:

Dried parsley, winter savory, sweet marjoram, lemon, thyme, of each two ounces; dried lemon peel and sweet basil, one ounce each; dry in a warm oven, pound, pass through a hair sieve, put it in a dry bottle and cork closely. It will retain its flavor a long time, and is a delicious flavoring.

Stock, or broth for soup, may be made from odds and ends of meat, poultry, game, knuckle of veal, shin of beef, etc.; pour over a small quantity of water at first, and cook very slow until the flavor and juices are extracted; add more water, flavor with herbs, vegetables, etc. Boil five or six hours slowly—some boil even longer. Let it cool over night. Skim off the fat, and it is ready for future use in soup.

CORN SOUP.

One old chicken, fat; twelve ears of corn, one-fourth pound of butter, one quart of milk. Boil the chicken in two quarts of water, and, when about half cooked, take it out and stuff and roast it. Cut the corn from the cob and put into the water in which the chicken has been boiled, (about three quarters of an hour before dinner) the butter, thickened with a little flour; just a few minutes before lifting, add the milk, pepper and salt to taste. As soon as it boils, serve.

POTATO SOUP.

Mrs. J. L. Watkins.

Two quarts water, six large potatoes, two quarts milk. Slice the potatoes very thin, and cook in the water until quite tender; add milk, one tablespoon of butter; pepper and salt to taste; thicken with a little flour stirred in cold milk. It should not be made very thick.

BEEF SOUP.

Take a small shin of beef, crack the bone, remove the tough outside skin; wash and put it on to boil in a kettle with six or eight quarts of water, and two tablespoonfuls of salt. After boiling perfectly tender, (which will take quite four hours,) take it out of the liquid, to which add more salt, if necessary; vegetables to your taste; one large tablespoonful of scorched sugar, a little sweet marjoram and thyme, (if liked,) and one small red pepper, cut in small pieces. Thicken very moderately with flour moistened with water to the consistency of cream, and stir in while boiling. About three quarters of an hour before the soup is served, put in eight medium sized potatoes, cut into quarters. Then make very small dumplings, with a quarter of a pound of flour, two ounces of butter, a little salt, and water to make a dough. Put into the soup and boil ten minutes. Last of all put in a little parsley, just before serving.

OYSTER SOUP.

Mrs. A. Pursell.

To one whole can of oysters take one and one-half pints water, and the same of good milk. Let the water and milk come to a boil; add half pound of butter, salt and pepper, and two tablespoonfuls corn starch. Pour in the oysters, and let them scald a few minutes.

OKRA SOUP.

Five quarts of water, two pounds of beef, two dozen okras, one dozen tomatoes, one teacupful of rice. Cut the okras in thin slices and boil a few minutes; pour off the water and add to the soup. Boil four hours. Season with salt, pepper and cloves.

VEGETABLE SOUP.

Four quarts of water, beef and bones, (the bones from roast beef and uncooked steak) two onions, two turnips, two tomatoes, two carrots, a piece of cabbage, all cut fine. Boil until all are tender, then remove the bones and meat, and season with salt, pepper and thyme.

RICE SOUP.

To three quarts of beef stock, add one onion, one teacupful of rice, one pint canned tomatoes. Season with salt and pepper.

MACARONI SOUP.

Six pounds of beef, four quarts of water, two onions, one pint of macaroni. When tender, remove the meat; add salt and pepper; the macaroni broken in pieces, and one tablespoonful of tomato catsup, and one of flour.

WHITE SOUP.

A large knuckle of veal, four quarts of water, a little celery, two onions, two carrots, two turnips. Boil down to two quarts; strain the liquor, and take off all the fat; add one pint of milk or cream, the beaten yolks of three eggs, and a little vermicelli. Let it boil a little, and serve.

TURKEY SOUP.

Crack the bones of cold roast turkey; boil in three quarts of water; add one cut onion, one turnip, a little rice, salt and pepper. When cooked sufficiently, strain. Add a little flour or boiled rice.

MUTTON SOUP.

Four quarts of water, three rounds of the fore quarter of mutton, two cut onions, two turnips, one-half can tomatoes, one teacupful of barley or rice. Boil four hours. Remove the meat and season with salt, pepper and thyme.

BEAN SOUP.

One pint of beans to two quarts of beef stock; soak the beans over night, and boil them soft. Add pepper and salt.

BRUNSWICK SOUP OR STEW.

Two chickens, five quarts water; boil until tender. Remove all the meat from the bones, pick it fine, and put it back into the broth after having taken off the fat. About two hours before dinner add six potatoes, chopped fine; after chopping them, boil separately for a few minutes; draw off the water before adding them to the soup. One quart or more of tomatoes, one pint of sweet corn, a little cayenne pepper, one tablespoonful Worcestershire sauce; salt to taste; add four hard boiled eggs—two chopped, two sliced. Before serving add one dozen small oyster crackers, one-half of them split. The corn and tomatoes should be added early enough to be thoroughly cooked. If the tomatoes are very sour, add one spoonful of sugar. Add eggs and crackers last.

FISH.

GENERAL DIRECTIONS.

In choosing fresh fish, the gills should be red, the eyes full, and the flesh firm and stiff; if a fish is flabby, the eyes sunk, and the gills pale, it is stale. Split the fish well open, clean out all blood—hold the head in your hand to scrape off the scales. Wash them as little as possible, and dry or drain them; never allow them to stand in water. A few minutes before cooking salt them; some prefer only to salt the water when they are boiled. Use very little water, cover tight; skim them; boil very gently. As soon as the flesh parts from the bone easily, they are done. Let the water be boiling before the fish is put in. Serve as soon as cooked, as the flavor of fish is injured by standing.

Eels should be glossy on the back and very white on the belly. Clean them well, skin them, and cut in pieces three or four inches long; let them stand an hour or more in salt water.

Olive oil is much used for frying fish. By straining it, it may be used more than once—any fat may be so used, and it becomes richer each time. Never use for meat, oil in which fish has been fried. Roll fish in eggs and bread crumbs, corn meal or flour.

TO BOIL SEA FISH (FRESH.)

Soak, some time before dressing, in cold water, in which throw a handful of salt; always notch the back before putting them in the kettle; salt the water, and let it heat gradually, boil gently, or they will break in pieces. A fish weighing eight pounds will boil in half an hour.

TO FRY SHAD.

Cut the fish in pieces, rinse and wipe dry; rub over the fish a little salt, and when it has melted, roll them in flour; heat the fat tried from salt pork, or oiled butter, nearly boiling hot; lay in the fish, the skin side up, fry until brown, and then turn them; cook slowly without burning. Serve plain. Horseradish makes a fine relish for fish.

TO FRY MACKEREL.

Take as many mackerel as are needed for the family, remove the skin, dip them in beaten eggs and bread crumbs, fry them slowly until done. For a sauce, pound the soft roes with sweet thick cream, and pass them through a sieve, melt some butter in a little real *consomme*, or water, if no *consomme* is at hand, stir in the cream and roes, add a little lemon juice and mushroom catsup, heat it hot, and pour it over the fish after it is dished.

HALIBUT STEAK.

Wash and wipe the steaks dry; have ready some rolled cracker or bread crumbs, then beat up two or three eggs; dip each steak into the beaten egg, then into the bread crumbs, (when you have salted the fish,) and fry in hot fat, lard, or nice dripping. Or, you can broil the steak upon a buttered gridiron, over a clear fire, first seasoning with salt and pepper.

STEWED COD FISH.

Soak the fish over night. Pick it into small pieces, not over an inch in size; stew until tender in plenty of water; pour off the water and season with pepper and butter; put in plenty of milk, and thicken with flour.

FRIED FISH.

Having cleaned the fish thoroughly, sprinkle with salt; let them stand a few hours, and wipe dry; dust thick with flour or corn meal; fry slowly, but have the fat boiling hot when the fish is put in the pan.

PICKLED SALMON.

Soak salt salmon twenty-four hours; pour boiling water over it to cook, but change water while cooking; melt butter, add two teaspoonfuls flour with two tablespoons of boiling water; add pepper, and pour over when ready for the table.

TO FRY BASS OR OTHER FRESH FISH.

After they have been cleansed, lay the pieces in a cloth to dry them; if convenient, fry four or five slices of pork, or else take lard and have it right hot; season the fish with a little salt and pepper, and dip in a dish of Indian meal and lay in the skillet; fry a nice brown, and serve hot.

TO BOIL FISH.

Dress them as for baking. Wrap them altogether in a cloth, or better still, put them in a clean bag and put the bag into boiling water. Let them boil half an hour. Pour over them, when dished, cream-gravy or drawn butter. I don't know which is best, baked or boiled fish; but no one but a dyspeptic, whose tastes are all morbid, will be likely to prefer fried fish to either. The best way to salt the fish is before cooking, if you have time, by letting them lay, already dressed, in a pan of salted water over night, or for an hour before dinner. Drain them from the salted water, or sprinkle salt over them if they have not been in salted water, and lay them in your clean dripping pan, and put them in the oven. They need about half-an-hour's good baking, and then you may pour over them a cup of creamy milk, and set them back in the oven for a few minutes. It is best to bake them in some baking-dish that will do to set upon the table just as it comes from the oven.

BROILED SHAD (FRESH).

Wash, wipe and split the fish, sprinkle with salt and pepper, and lay it upon a buttered gridiron, inside downward; when the lower side is browned, turn the fish. One of medium size will be done in about twenty minutes. Serve upon a hot dish, and lay a good piece of butter upon the fish.

BROILED SHAD (SALT).

Soak over night in lukewarm water. Take out in the morning and put it into ice cold water for half an hour. Broil as you do fresh shad. Mackerel may be done the same way.

FRIED CAT FISH.

Scald and clean the fish, sprinkle with salt, and keep in a cool place several hours. Dip the fish in grated cracker, meal or flour, and fry quickly in hot lard. Take up as soon as done.

SALT CODFISH.

Soak the fish in water over night, put in fresh water with a little soda, let it keep warm, but not boil; change the water an hour before dinner, and let it scald; take out the fish, and dress with egg sauce.

DIRECTIONS FOR FRYING FROGS.
Mrs. McGinley.

For 1 doz. frogs, take ¼ pound of crackers, roll very fine; then take 3 eggs, beat very light; add a very little water (cold) then pepper and salt; dip the frog in the egg, then cover with cracker; then drop them in boiling butter; fry till a light brown.

Sauces for Fish.

SAUCE FOR TRIPE, HERRING AND LOBSTERS.

Two tablespoons of mustard to a quarter of a pint of butter. This is a nice sauce.

DRAWN BUTTER SAUCE.

Half a pint of boiling water; two teaspoonfuls of flour; two ounces of butter; mix the flour and butter together until they are perfectly smooth; stir this into the boiling water, and add salt to taste. If made with milk in place of water, less butter will answer.

EGG SAUCE.

This is made like drawn butter, with the addition of three eggs, boiled hard and chopped fine. Nice sauce for fish.

OYSTERS.

OYSTER PIE.

Line a deep dish with pie-crust, put in the bottom a layer of fine cracker or bread crumbs, then add the oysters, a part of one quart, with pieces of butter, and a little salt and pepper, and a part of the liquor from the oysters. Over the oysters, put a layer of crackers or bread crumbs, season as above and add the remainder of the liquor, and cover with pie crust. Cut a hole in the top of the crust, and bake one hour slowly. Serve hot.

ESCALOPED OYSTERS.
Mrs. A. McFarland.

Butter a deep dish, and cover the bottom with fine bread crumbs or rolled crackers. Put in a layer of oysters, and add bits of butter, salt and pepper, then another layer of crumbs, and so on till the dish is full. Pour part of the liquor over the above. Bake one quart of oysters half an hour. Have crumbs on the top dish.

HOW TO PICKLE OYSTERS FOR LUNCH.

Cook them until they burst open, strain off the liquid, add vinegar, allspice and whole black pepper. Let them stand for a day.

FRIED OYSTERS.

Dip them in batter made of eggs and bread crumbs; season with nutmeg, mace and salt. Fry in lard until brown.

FRIED OYSTERS.

Take the largest oysters from their liquor and lay them on a clean cloth, to absorb the moisture. Have ready several beaten eggs and crackers, crushed fine. In the frying pan heat enough nice butter to cover the oysters entirely. Dip each oyster first in the egg, then in the cracker, rolling it over, that it may become completely incrusted. Drop them carefully into the frying pan and fry quickly, to a light brown. Do not let them lie in the pan an instant after they are done.

 MEATS.

GENERAL DIRECTIONS.

The great point in cooking meats is to have them tender, without wasting the juices.

Most cooks think hard boiling necessary; on the contrary, by simmering slowly in as little water as possible, the meat will be more savory and tender.

In boiling, allow from eighteen to twenty minutes to every pound of meat.

Put fresh meat in hot, salted meat in cold, water.

Never let meat stand in the water after it is done.

Save all liquors in which meats have been boiled for soup.

Skim off all scum rising—you may aid it in rising by throwing in a very little cold water.

The sirloin is best for roasting.

The round is best for boiling.

For steak, the inside of the sirloin is considered best; cut about three-fourths of an inch thick.

Frying is considered the poorest way of cooking meat, as the hot fat renders them indigestible. Broiled or baked steak is better.

Use the suet to fry steak; it is healthier than any other fat.

The juice which flows from the meat is the best gravy. Season, and if too thin, sift in a little flour; if too greasy, skim.

HEAD CHEESE.

This is made of the head, ears and tongue. Boil in salted water until tender; remove the bones and chop fine. Season with salt, pepper and sage, with a little vinegar. Mix all together thoroughly; pack in bowl; press down by putting a plate on the top; (first wet the plate;) in a day's time this will be ready for use. This is generally eaten cold for tea, with vinegar and mustard, but can be cut in slices, seasoned slightly with mustard, and warmed in a frying pan with enough butter to prevent burning.

TO BOIL A HAM.

One weighing twelve pounds should boil five or six hours. A very nice way to cook a ham is to boil it half the time it takes to cook it, then take off the skin and cover the fat side with grated cracker or bread crumbs, and lay it into a dripping pan. Let it cook the remainder of the time. In cooking it in this way, the ham is much sweeter and more delicate.

TO FRY HAM AND EGGS.

Cut your ham thin and take off the rind; if very salty, pour hot water over the slices, but do not let it remain long, as it spoils the taste of the meat; wipe dry and lay in a hot skillet, and turn in a minute or two. The secret of frying ham nicely is to do it quickly. Never put the slices in until the skillet is hot, and, when done, lay on a warm dish. Break your eggs seperately into the skillet, after the ham has been removed, and as they begin to fry, dip the boiling fat over them until they are done. This prevents the necessity of turning them. Serve hot.

SAUSAGES.

The proper seasoning is salt, pepper, sage, summer savory, or thyme. They should be one-third fat, the remainder lean, finely chopped, and the seasonings well mixed and proportioned, so that one herb may not predominate over the others. If skins are used, they cannot be prepared with too much care; but they are about as well made into cakes. Spread the cakes on a clean, white-wood board, and keep them in a dry, cool place. Fry them long and gently. Serve with potatoes, plain stewed apples, without sugar, baked sour apples, or sour pickles.

LARD.

Leaf lard is the nicest for all cooking purposes. Skin all the fat that is to be tried into lard, and commence by frying gently a little leaf lard, or your fat will scorch; let it cook slowly, and dip off the fat as fast as it is liquified, and strain it through a cloth; when all is strained that can be dipped off, squeeze the remainder by itself in the cloth. If the lard is to be used for cooking, salt it a trifle; but, if for burning in lard lamps, salt would be injurious. If the fat is not skinned before trying, the gluten in the skin will make the lard impure and frothy. Save the scraps and skins for soap grease.

SUPERIOR PORK AND BEANS.

Look over the beans and put them to soak the evening previous to cooking, in soft water; parboil and throw off the water twice; prepare a piece of pork and put it in the beans with the third water; let the water boil up; skim and boil five minutes, and drain both pork and beans thoroughly. Have ready boiling water; put the beans and pork in the pot with as little water as will cover them; simmer gently until tender. The water should all be evaporated when done, leaving the beans nearly dry. Taste, and if not sufficiently salted by the pork, season with more, but be careful not to get too much salt. Spread the beans evenly in a baking dish; slash the pork and put it on a pan by itself to bake; it should be handsomely browned. Stir up the beans often, until within twenty minutes of dinner time, then spread them evenly and let them brown. If they do not look sufficiently brown, wet them over with egg, and brown with hot iron or any other manner convenient. Lay the pork in the middle, without the fat which dripped from it in roasting. This will be found much more healthy than when prepared after the old rule of baking pork and beans in the same dish. Horse-radish, catsups and pickles are the best relishes.

Stewed beans are prepared as above, and gently boiled in the last water with the pork until nearly dry. Beans should be cooked in soft water, or, if hard, with a small bit of soda in the water.

SUPERIOR BEEF TO USE COLD FROM POOR PIECES.

Soak in warm, not hot water, until fresh as desired when boiled. Then cover it with water, and boil slowly; skim the pot as long as any scum rises, after which cover the pot closely, that the condensed steam may fall in the pot, and boil steadily, until the meat will break into bits if lifted with a fork; when sufficiently tender, skim it out, remove the bone, and mix the fat and lean together, put in a wide earthen dish, deep enough to hold it; skim the fat from the liquor, and boil the liquor down; when sufficiently reduced, pour it over the meat; lay over it a flat cover, and put on a weight of fifteen or twenty pounds, and let it stand all night. When wanted for the table, cut in thin slices, as you would head-cheese. The jelly of the liquor will make it firm, and if properly mixed the fat and the lean will be in right proportion through the whole. This is an excellent way to manage the poor pieces of corned beef. The gristle will be tender, and every part good. The gelatine of the muscles will be saved; though not considered particularly nutritious when used alone, it will assist in forming the meat into a solid mass, making it both agreeable to the eye and taste. If the beef is much salt, it should be soaked forty-eight hours, or longer if not sufficiently freshened, to allow all the water to evaporate, and the jelly to solidify, without tasting too much of the brine.

TO COOK DRIED BEEF.

Slice it as thin as possible, and let it lie in water, over night, or less time, if not very salt. Stew it in water sufficient to make the gravy needed, until tender. Beat up an egg with a little flour; add a lump of butter to the beef, and stir in the egg and flour. Toast bread; lay the beef nicely on it, and pour the gravy over it; add a trifle of pepper at the table, if relished.

TO CORN BEEF.
Mrs. Towne.

6 gallons of water, 10 lbs of salt, 2½ oz. saltpetre, 3 lbs sugar or 1 qt. molasses, ½ oz soda. Boiled and skimmed, will cover about one hundred lbs. of beef.

BEEF TONGUE SALAD.

Boil one beef tongue perfectly tender, grate fine; the yolks of four hard-boiled eggs, mashed fine, with two table spoonfuls of olive oil, add 1 tablespoonful of mustard, 1½ teaspoonfuls of salt, and enough vinegar to mix dressing with, and mix altogether.

SPICED BEEF.
Mrs. M. B. Ross.

2 lbs. of lean beef, chopped very fine; 9 milk crackers rolled fine; 4 eggs well beaten, mix altogether thoroughly; seasoned high; place it in bread tins, put thin pieces of butter or pork over the top; bake 1 hour.

TO COOK A STEAK.

Take a tender steak, well pounded or scored; season with salt and pepper. Have the skillet *quite* hot, put in the steak, and with a knife, keep stirring it about and pressing it, until it is very juicy, then cover closely for a few minutes; turn it over and let it cook a very few minutes longer. Have your platter ready, heated and buttered. Put your steak on this, and a few pieces of butter on the steak. Set it in the oven until the butter melts, when it is ready for the table. The meat thus cooked, in its own juice, seems much sweeter than any other way.

MEAT CAKES.
Mrs. W. A. Hutchins.

Chop pieces of cold steak or roast, add equal quantity of chopped potato, season with pepper and salt; make into small cakes, and fry for breakfast or tea. Very nice. Add onion if you like.

FRIED LIVER.

Cut the liver in slices half an inch thick; pour boiling water over and let stand five minutes. Season with salt and pepper and dredge with flour. Fry in hot grease, a nice brown. Make gravy of flour and milk.

DIRECTIONS FOR ROASTING A QUARTER OF LAMB.

Paper the roast all over, baste frequently, and cook thoroughly; if underdone, it is not fit to eat; when sufficiently roasted, the gravy which drops from it is entirely free from color; remove the paper half an hour before taking it from the fire; dredge it with flour and baste it with butter until it has penetrated the meat; brown nicely. The first basting liquid should be prepared with a little butter, salt and pepper, to season the meat. Some advise to cut off the fore shoulder and lift the flesh with a fork, and season it with pepper, salt, butter, and a little lemon juice. If done, the shoulder must be replaced neatly, so as not to mar the quarter. It is easier to run a knife in the flesh in several places, making openings without removing any of the flesh, and dust in pepper, salt and lemon juice, if relished. Serve with mint sauce, the gravy of the quarter, or plain. Asparagus, peas and potatoes are the vegetables proper for serving with lamb; for relishes, use salads.

LAMB CHOPS.

Fry them a light brown, in butter; then add a little water, flour, salt, and a dust of pepper to the gravy. Let it brown, and pour it over the chops.

BROILED LAMB STEAK.

Broil slowly until quite done; then make a gravy with fresh butter, melted by the steak; add a dust of pepper and a little salt, dissolved in a tablespoon of water. Serve with peas, potatoes and salads.

LAMB CUTLETS.

Trim the slices free from fat, beat up the yolk of egg with grated bread crumbs or crackers; season with pepper and salt; dip in the cutlets and fry in butter or lard, gently, until thoroughly done.

TO BOIL A LEG OF MUTTON.

Cut off the bone close to the flesh, and nicely trim the knuckle; pour over it milk, boiling hot, and let it lay until the milk is cold; cover it with cold water in the stewpan, add salt, and simmer gently until done. Remove the scum as fast as it rises to the surface of the water. It will take from two to two and a half hours to boil. Serve with boiled turnips, onions, potatoes and caper sauce; if the caper sauce is not to be had, make a sauce of drawn butter, flavored with celery.

VEAL LOAF.
Mrs. Hickok.

Three pounds of veal, raw, lean; one-half pound salt pork, both chopped fine, without cooking; six Boston crackers, rolled; three eggs well beaten, one teaspoonful pepper, one teaspoon salt, one teaspoonful thyme; press hard in a dish; bake three hours. Nice sliced cold for tea.

VEAL PIE.

Prepare a plain paste, cover a deep plate with it; set it in the oven until baked; have ready veal that has been parboiled; cut in small bits; lay the meat on the crust until it is evenly full; put in each pie a piece of butter as large as the bowl of a tablespoon, broken into small bits, a little salt and pepper, a spoonful of flour, and a little of the broth in which the veal was boiled. Put on the top crust, which should be made richer than the bottom, and rolled thin; bake immediately in a quick oven. Serve with potatoes and any other dressed vegetables.

VEAL LOAF.
Mrs. M. B. Ross.

Three pounds veal, chopped fine, eight crackers, well rolled; mix with the meat; salt and pepper well, and a good quantity of butter. Pack it in a basin, cover, and bake three hours; half an hour before it is done, take off the cover and let the top brown. When cold, cut in slices.

CREAM OMELET.

Five eggs; three tablespoonfuls of cream; beat the whites and yolks separately; add the cream to the yolks; then join the whites quickly to the yolks and cream, with salt, and a very little parsley, if desired; have your pan ready, put in a lump of butter, and set it over the fire; pour the omelet into the pan just as the butter is boiling; when cooked, lay the omelet together, and serve.

DELICATE OMELET.

Six eggs, the whites beaten to a stiff froth, and the yolks well beaten; a teacupful of warm milk, with a tablespoonful of butter melted in it; a tablespoonful of flour, wet to a paste with a little of the milk, and poured to the milk; a teaspoonful of salt and a little cayenne pepper; mix all except the whites—add those last; have your griddle very hot and well greased; drop in a large spoonful; as soon as brown, turn over and serve immediately.

OMELET.

4 eggs; 1 pint of milk; 1 tablespoonful of corn starch or flour; a small lump of butter, with a little pepper and salt; beat well, and put it in a pan in the oven for 15 or 20 minutes.

Or, 6 well-beaten eggs; 12 tablespoonfuls of milk or cream; a lump of butter half the size of an egg; salt and pepper to the taste; put all in a bright, buttered pan, and set it into or over the steam of boiling water; scrape it from the pan till it thickens, and serve immediately.

HAM OMELET.
Mrs. W. A. Hutchins.

Stir teacup of chopped cold ham in six well-beaten eggs; season with pepper and salt.

BUTTERED EGGS.

Two slices of toast; two eggs; four tablespoonfuls of milk; sprinkle pepper and salt on the toast; beat the eggs lightly; put the milk over the fire, and when warm stir in the eggs; continue stirring, until as thick as cream; take it off the fire and stir it for a minute longer, then turn it on the buttered toast, and sprinkle with pepper and salt.

POACHED EGGS.

Have on the fire a pan of water fast boiling; break each egg into a cup, and slip carefully into the water; when the white is set the eggs are done; take them up on a slice, and serve on toast or bread and butter.

STUFFED EGGS.

Take out yolks of hard boiled eggs, mix with them some light bread crumbs, softened with milk; season well with butter, salt and pepper; fill the whites of the eggs with the seasoning; put in pan, pour milk over them, and put them in an oven to brown.

TO BOIL EGGS.

To try the freshness of eggs, put them into a pan of cold water—those that sink are the best; always let the water boil before putting the eggs in; three minutes will boil them soft; four minutes will cook the whites completely, and in six minutes they will be sufficiently hard for garnishing salads and dishes requiring them.

TO FRY EGGS.

Proceed exactly as for poaching, only instead of water, use butter or bacon.

SAUCE.

ONION SAUCE.

Boil some large onions in a good deal of water till they are tender; put them in a cullender, and when drained, pass them through it with a spoon; put them in a sauce pan with a good piece of butter, a little salt, and a gill of cream; stir them over the fire until they are of a good thickness.

TOMATO SAUCE.

6 nice ripe tomatoes; squeeze out the seeds; stew until soft with four tablespoonfuls of gravy or broth; pass through a sieve; season with cayenne pepper; if too thick, add more gravy; butter may be used instead of gravy.

CELERY SAUCE FOR FOWLS.

1 bunch of celery cut fine and boiled tender; add half-pint of cream and a small piece of butter rolled in flour; boil all gently.

MUSTARD SAUCE.

Mrs. A. V. Sappington.

5 yolks of eggs; 5 teaspoons mustard; 5 teaspoons sugar; 1 teaspoon allspice; 1 teaspoon cayenne pepper; 1 tumbler currant jelly; 2 tumblers vinegar; (one cup of butter, if you like;) put it on cold; stir constantly, cook a minute or two; pour in a jar, let it cool, and set in the cellar or some cool place.

Poultry and Game.

GENERAL DIRECTIONS.

Poultry should be plump, but not too fat.

If the skin is full of coarse hairs, it is old.

Lift the wing of a fowl, if young and tender, it will tear easily; if it is very hard to break the skin, the fowl is old.

Be careful to cook poultry well, nothing is worse than the taste and appearance half done.

Be careful not to break the gall bladder; you cannot wash away the bitter.

To make an old fowl tender, put a tablespoonful of lemon juice in the water in which you boil it. Strong vinegar will do, but is not so good.

If game smells strong, wash it in vinegar and water.

Birds can be kept longer by plunging them, after they are cleaned, into boiling water five or six minutes; then salt and pepper inside; wash them off before cooking.

Cook slices of bacon with pigeons and rabbits.

BOILED CHICKEN POT-PIE.

Take one quart of flour, three teaspoonfuls of baking powder, half cup of lard, a little salt, and mix with water; roll the dough and cut in square pieces. Cut up a chicken in all the joints, peel and quarter eight or ten potatoes, place some chicken and potatoes in the vessel, season with salt and pepper, and lumps of butter; over this place some of the squares of dough; repeat this until all the chicken and potatoes are used, having dough on top. Fill the vessel with boiling water and boil two hours.

CHICKEN PIE.

Prepare your chicken as for stewed chicken for the table; add some small bits of dough; make a rich gravy of milk, butter, salt, pepper and flour; prepare your crust as for pastry; line your pan, if you like, with the crust. Add a top crust and bake quickly.

PIE CRUST.
Mrs. J. C. Gilbert.

Three coffee cups of flour, one teacup of shortening, a teaspoonful of salt; cut with a knife till very fine; add water enough to wet it up, and roll thin.

TO ROAST A DUCK OR GOOSE.

Add to the usual stuffing of bread crumbs, pepper, salt, &c., a tablespoon of melted butter, a large-sized onion, chopped fine, a tablespoonful of chopped sage; mix these with the yolks of two eggs; stuff and sew up; baste well. The giblets should be stewed in a very little water, then chopped fine and add to the gravy in the dripping pan, with a spoonful of browned flour. Serve with currant jelly.

TO ROAST A TURKEY.
Mrs. A. Pursell.

Having secured a nice tender turkey, see that it is well washed; salt and pepper inside, cut in small pieces stale bread, salt and pepper, two tablespoons of sage, (after it has been rubbed fine,) two eggs and a lump of butter as large as an egg; over this mixture pour boiling water, to moisten, (not wet;) stuff turkey; salt and pepper outside; dust flour, and roast about three or four hours, according to size.

TO PREPARE A TURKEY FOR COOKING.
Mrs. John N. Lodwick.

Salt and pepper, rubbed on inside and outside; dry bread crumbs, salt, pepper and butter; mix well together; rub outside of fowl with butter, put in oven without water, bake brown; then sprinkle a tablespoonful of flour, add one pint of water, and baste well until it is done.

A fillet of veal can be prepared and cooked in like manner.

TO ROAST A TURKEY.

Proceed as directed in roast fowls; allow from two and a half to three hours for a good-sized, tender turkey. The dressing of fowls can be varied by using oysters.

TO ROAST A PHEASANT.

To roast a pheasant, proceed exactly as in roasting a fowl; allow from forty to fifty minutes for a full grown pheasant. Serve with browned gravy, acid jelly and dressed potatoes.

TO ROAST QUAIL.

Pick them with great care, and draw them so as to leave all the fat in the bodies of the birds; wash and dry them nicely; stuff them with bread moistened with melted butter and a very little water, seasoned with pepper and salt; truss them nicely; and fasten the wings and legs in place with very small skewers, roast or bake them fifteen or twenty minutes, basting frequently. Toast some nice bread quickly on both sides, without burning; make up the gravy from the drippings; soak the toast, lay the slices in order on the platter, allowing half a slice to each bird; remove the skewers and strings, set a bird on each half slice of toast, and dip the gravy over them. Serve hot. When the birds are roasted without stuffing, they will cook in from ten to fifteen minutes.

JELLIED CHICKEN.

Mrs. W. A. Hutchins.

To six well boiled, boned, and chopped chickens, allow one box of Cox's gelatine, soaked, until dissolved, in one quart of cold water; when the chicken is ready, add gelatine, and also the broth in which the chickens were boiled, which should be about three pints after boiling down; season to taste. Put in deep dish, and turn out when cold.

Soup meat prepared in the same way, leaving out the gelatine.

TO ROAST A FOWL.

Having nicely dressed the fowl, have ready a dressing seasoned with pepper, salt and summer savory; fill the body of the bird, sew up the opening, truss it nicely, oil it with butter, and put it before a moderately hot, but bright fire, or hot oven; heat the skin evenly as soon as possible; cover it with paper if there is the least danger of its browning too soon; roast pretty fast, without scorching, the first half hour, and baste the fowl all over every five minutes; after this, let it roast steadily, but rather slowly, three-quarters of an hour, when, if young and tender, it will be done quite through. Stick a fork through the breast and thigh, and if the fluid which follows the fork is entirely free from blood, it is done. If not browned, replenish the fire, wet the fowl over with a very little yolk of egg, dust it lightly with flour, and let it brown evenly all over. Remove the skewers and strings before sending it to the table.

TO ROAST A PARTRIDGE.

Prepare the bird and roast it in every respect as a fowl; when quite done, remove it from the fire; game is ruined if overdone. A young partridge will roast in from twenty to twenty-five minutes, and an old one may take forty minutes.

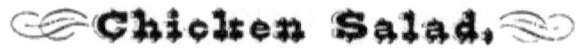

Chicken Salad.

CHICKEN SALAD.
Mrs. H. A. Towne.

4 chickens; 8 bunches of celery; 8 eggs (yolks only) well beaten; 1 tablespoonful sugar; 1 tablespoonful salt; 2 tablespoonfuls prepared mustard; a little cayenne pepper; ½ cup sweet cream; 1 pint of vinegar; 1 cup of butter or olive oil; boil together, stirring constantly, and pour over chicken and celery.

CHICKEN SALAD.
Mrs. E. R. Moore.

2 large fowls boiled. Yolks of 9 hard eggs; ½ pint table oil; ½ pint vinegar; 1 gill mixed mustard; 1 teaspoonful cayenne pepper; 1 teaspoonful salt; 2 large heads of cabbage cut fine; pick chicken fine; celery will improve it.

CHICKEN SALAD.
Mrs. Rhodes.

2 large chickens, boiled and chopped; 2 large celery heads cut with knife; 1 pint vinegar; 1 tablespoon flour; 2 tablespoons milk; 2 tablespoons mustard; yolks of three eggs; pepper and salt to taste; ½ cup butter; stir egg and seasoning together, pour the vinegar, boiling, on them—to be stirred into the salad when cold.

CHICKEN SALAD.

Mrs. Dunlevy.

1 common sized fowl; ½ cup olive oil; ¼ jar French mustard; ½ pint vinegar; yolks of five hard-boiled eggs; 1 teaspoon cayenne pepper; 8 stalks celery; salt; put dressing on just before serving.

CHICKEN SALAD.

Miss Mary Terry.

To two chickens chopped fine, take nine hard boiled eggs; chop the whites with two large heads of celery; mix with the chickens 1 gill of mustard, 1 tablespoonful of pepper, salt to taste; then take the yolks of the eggs, make soft with ½ pint of vinegar, ½ pint of melted butter.

VEGETABLES.

GENERAL DIRECTIONS.

Vegetables should be freshly gathered. Those that are wilted, may be freshened by letting them stand in cold water a short time before cooking.

Soft water is best; if you have to use hard water, use a very small bit of soda, or carbonate of ammonia; be careful of the soda, too much spoils the flavor. Always use plenty of water, and boil fast. Always have water to pour off, never let it cook down on any vegetable.

Put vegetables on in boiling water.

Never cook two kinds in one kettle, unless intending to serve them in the same dish.

Never let them stand a minute in the water after they are done.

Potatoes, when boiled, should always be carefully dried before serving.

BAKED EGG PLANT.
Mrs. Powell.

Take two moderate sized egg plants, or one large one; boil till soft, and squeeze well; then take off the skin; chop it, and put through a cullender, to extract as much of the water as possible. Take a small loaf of stale bread, grate it fine; 3 hard boiled eggs chopped fine; mix them with the bread and ¼ lb. of butter; then mix the egg plant in well; season it highly with pepper and salt. Put it in a deep dish: grate bread over the top to form a crust, and lay some pieces of butter over it. Bake and serve hot.

TO FRY EGG PLANT.

Cut the egg plant in slices, not quite half an inch thick; put them in salt and water for one hour; then take them out and wipe dry; pepper them, and dip them in boiling lard, and then in bread crumbs; put them back in the boiling lard, and fry a light brown. Sprinkle salt over them after they are fried. Serve hot.

SALSIFY DRESSED AS OYSTERS.

Wash and scrape salsify (as much as will be needed,) and boil it until perfectly soft, but not broken. Mash it, and season with butter; pepper and salt to your taste. Beat the yolks of three eggs, very light; crumb a stale loaf of baker's bread, and season with salt and pepper. Have ready a pan of hot lard and butter mixed; take a spoonful of the plant, dip it into the egg, cover it with the crumbs, and drop it into the pan to fry. When the under side is done, put some egg and bread over the top, turn it, and fry a light brown. Serve hot, for breakfast or dinner.

YOUNG ONION (STEWED.)

Peel thirty young onions, all of a size; boil until tender; put them into half a pint of melted butter, and half pint milk. Season with salt.

TO COOK PARSNIPS.

Scrape and wash the parsnips, and slice them lengthwise; boil in just enough water to cover them, until thoroughly done; drain off the water, put in a piece of butter, pepper and salt. Beat up an egg with one-half cup of milk, pour over them and serve hot.

TO COOK ASPARAGUS.
Mrs. S. L. Watkins.

2 qts. of water, salt, and a piece of soda as large as a pea; let the water boil; put in the asparagus, after first scraping the hard ends; when tender, which will be in one-half an hour, generally, pour off all the water; season with butter, pepper, and plenty of milk, thickened a little.

STEWED ONIONS.

Leave the onions whole, or slice them, as is wished; put plenty of cold water on; when half done, pour it off and pour over boiling water; when tender, pour off the water, and dress with milk, thickened with flour; season to taste. Onions cooked in this way, will agree with delicate stomachs.

MACARONI.
S. E. F.

Cover the bottom of the dish with macaroni, boiled soft, then a layer of grated cheese, seasoned with mustard, pepper and salt, and so on, until the dish is full; if wanted very rich, add a little butter, then bake in a moderate oven.

COLD SLAW.
Mrs. M. B. Ross.

Shave your cabbage into fine slips; beat up two eggs, add to this one gill of vinegar and water mixed; put it on the fire; when it begins to thicken, stir in a piece of butter, a little salt, and a teaspoonful of sugar. When cold, pour over the cabbage.

CABBAGE SALAD.
Mrs. M. B. Ross.

3 eggs well beaten; 1 teacup vinegar; 2 tablespoons mustard; 1 teaspoon of salt; 1 teaspoon pepper; 1 tablespoon butter. Let this mixture come to a boil, and when cool, add 7 tablespoons of cream. Half a cabbage, shaved fine.

COLD SLAW.

Cut the cabbage fine, with a slaw cutter, and then prepare the following: one heaping teaspoonful each of prepared mustard and salt, two tablespoonfuls of cream, one tablespoonful of butter, three tablespoonfuls of sugar, two-thirds of a cup of vinegar, yolks of two eggs, well beaten; stir all together, and set on the fire, stirring constantly until it thickens, then pour over the cabbage.

COLD SLAW.
Mrs. W. A. Hutchins.

Half head of prepared cabbage, tablespoonful of prepared mustard, teaspoonful sugar, pepper and salt, and the yolk of one egg well beaten, and stir in a cup of boiling vinegar and water. Mix well together, and cover for a few minutes.

DELICIOUS SLAW.

½ head of cabbage, cut fine; 1 large stalk of celery, cut fine; a hard boiled egg, 2 oz. grated horseradish, and 2 teaspoonfuls of mustard. Mix with vinegar, pepper and salt, to taste.

FRIED RICE.

1 pint of cold boiled rice; 2 eggs, beat light; 3 tablespoons flour; 1 pint of milk. Salt and pepper, fry in cakes on a griddle.

PRESERVING CORN.

To 24 lbs. of corn (cut from cob,) add 6 qts. of water, 3 oz. tartaric acid; dissolve the acid in the water before putting with the corn. Let it scald well, then can and make air tight.

FRIED CORN.

Mrs. J. L. Watkins.

6 ears of corn, 1 cup milk, 2 eggs beat light, salt and pepper. Slice off the outer edge of the grain, and then scrape the heart from the corn, leaving the husks on the cob as much as possible. Melt one tablespoon of butter in a skillet; mix all the ingredients together, and pour them in. Cover tight and cook very slow—stirring frequently to prevent burning.

BAKED TOMATOES.

Six smooth tomatoes; salt and pepper; butter and sugar; six pieces of buttered toast. Peel the tomatoes, place the pieces of toast in the dish in which you bake them; place a tomato on each piece of toast, (not having the pieces too large,) put a piece of butter the size of a nutmeg on each tomato, also two or three tablespoonfuls of sugar, scattered over them with the salt, and pepper. Bake one hour and a half, in a moderate oven. Serve hot.

BAKED TOMATOES.

Mrs. E. Glover.

Take a shallow pan, put a layer of tomatoes, sliced thin; cover this with bread crumbs; butter, pepper, salt; sugar or not, as you like; then another layer of tomatoes, ending with the bread, &c. on top. Bake in a slow oven three-fourths of an hour.

TO FRY TOMATOES.

Cut some tomatoes in slices; mix some corn meal, pepper and salt; roll the slices of tomatoes well in the mixture; have about a tablespoonful of lard, boiling hot, in the spider, and fry them crisp and brown. If desired to have them very rich, put a small piece of butter with each slice of tomato.

TO CAN TOMATOES AND CORN.

Take one-third of the quantity of tomatoes that you do corn; cut the corn from the cob and scald and can.

BAKED CORN.

Prepare exactly as for fried corn ; place in a vessel and bake ; beat the white of egg separately and stir in last. This should bake slow. Will take about three-fourths of an hour to one hour.

STEWED CORN.

Split the grains and scrape from the cob, letting the husk remain ; stew with very little water, merely enough to prevent burning ; cook slow ; season with thickened milk, butter, pepper, salt. Children and invalids who can not eat corn any other way, will find it to agree with them, by being careful to split the grains and scrape well.

GREEN CORN PUDDING.
Mrs. C. G. Young.

Cut half the grain of two dozen ears tender young corn, and scrape the balance with a knife ; 5 eggs, well beaten ; 1 pint rich milk : ¼ lbs. butter ; salt and pepper to taste ; stir a tablespoonful of flour into the milk until smooth, then add eggs, corn and melted butter. Bake in a tin pan.

CORN OYSTERS.
Mary E. Draper.

1 pint grated corn ; 1 small teacup flour ; ½ teacup butter ; salt and pepper ; mix well and fry a light brown.

CORN PUDDING.

One dozen ears of corn, cut or grated ; half doz. eggs ; 1 pint milk : ¼ lb. butter ; pepper and salt. Bake half an hour.

TO BROWN POTATOES WITH MEAT.

Boil some nice large potatoes, take off the skins carefully, and about an hour before the meat is done, put them into the dripping pan, having well dredged them with flour. Drain them from any grease, and serve hot.

TO MASH POTATOES.

Potatoes; a piece of butter the size of an egg; two tablespoonfuls of cream; salt. Prepare the potatoes nicely by paring and washing; put into a vessel, with a teaspoonful of salt, and cold water enough to cover them; let them boil half an hour, or until tender; then drain the water from them and mash them fine with a potato pestle; add the butter, and cream, and salt to the potato; mix until thoroughly incorporated, and they have become a smooth mash; put the mash into a dish, and smooth with a knife, and spread over the top, the yolk of an egg, and place in the oven long enough to brown nicely. Serve hot.

GREEN PEAS.

Boil, in salted water, a little more than enough to cover them, from fifteen to thirty minutes, according to their age; add butter and more salt, if needed, and boil up once. When old, they are improved by putting a very little saleratus into the water in which they are boiled, say a quarter of a teaspoonful to half a peck of shelled peas.

GREEN PEAS WITH CREAM.

Two quarts of green peas; boil fifteen or twenty minutes; when done, drain off the water; season with salt and pepper, a small lump of butter, and a teacup of cream. Serve hot.

GREEN PEAS.

Cook in plenty of water, a small piece of soda and a teaspoon of sugar; pour all the water off, and thicken with milk and flour. Season with butter, pepper and salt.

BAKED POTATOES.

Take as many large and equal sized potatoes as you wish; wash them nicely, and wipe dry; then put them in a quick oven for one hour. Serve as soon as done.

COOKING BEANS.

Moore's Rural New Yorker.

"If, my dear *Rural*, you ever should wish
For breakfast or dinner a tempting dish
Of the beans so famous in Boston town,
You must read the rules I here lay down:
When the sun has set in golden light,
And around you fall the shades of night,
A large deep dish, you first prepare,
A quart of beans select with care;
And pick them over, until you find
Not a speck or a moat is left behind;
A lot of cold water on them pour
'Till every bean is covered o'er,
And they seem to your poetic eye
Like pearls in the depths of the sea to lie;
Here, if you please, you may let them stay
'Till just after breakfast the very next day,
When a parboiling process must be gone through,
(I mean for the beans and not for you;)
Then, if in the pantry there still should be
That bean pot, so famous in history,
With all due deference bring it out
And, if there's a skimmer lying about,
Skim half of the beans from the boiling pan
Into the bean pot, as fast as you can;
Then turn to Biddy and calmly tell her
To take a huge knife and go to the cellar—
For you must have, like Shylock of old,
"A pound of flesh," ere your beans grow cold;
But, very unlike that ancient Jew,
Nothing but pork will do for you;
Then tell once more your maiden fair,
In the choice of the piece to take great care,
For a streak of fat and a streak of lean

Will give the right flavor to every bean!
This you must wash, and rinse, and score,
Put into the pot, and round it pour
The rest, till the view presented seems
Like an island of pork in an ocean of beans;
Pour on boiling water enough to cover
The tops of the beans completely over,
Shove in the oven and bake till done,
And the triumph of Yankee cooking's done."

MASHED POTATOES.

When the potatoes are thoroughly boiled, drain off the water; add salt and butter, and mash and stir with a potato masher; then add some sweet milk, and stir until the potatoes are both white and light.

SARATOGA POTATOES.
Mrs. Mary E. Draper.

Pare the potatoes and let them lie in very cold water four or five hours, then slice very thin with a potato slicer. Have ready a skillet, two-thirds full of hot lard; take a handful at a time and dry between the folds of a soft cloth; when dry, put them into the lard, stirring continually with a fork, to keep the slices separated. Fry a light brown. Place in a cullender to drain, and sprinkle a little salt over them.

TO FRY POTATOES CRISP.

Peel and slice the potatoes very thin, and fry in boiling lard, a few at a time; salt them as fast as fried, and set them in the oven to keep hot until all are finished. Send to the table in a covered dish.

FRIED POTATOES.

Take cold mashed potatoes; make in small cakes; flour on both sides, and fry in butter until brown on each side.

YEAST.

RISING.

A little brown sugar added to yeast will make bread or biscuit rise quickly.

YEAST.

Parboil and mash 6 large potatoes; 1 pint of boiling (hop) water, and 1 pint of cold water; strain this through a cullender and add 1 teacup of sugar, 1 tablespoonful of salt, 1 teaspoonful of ginger, and when cool, 1 teacup of good yeast; let it rise, and then bottle it, always shaking up well before using it.

YEAST.
Mrs. A. L. Martin.

3½ pints of water; 1 handful of hops; 1 tablespoon salt; 1 tablespoon of ginger; 1 teacup of sugar; boil this together; 8 large potatoes grated; stir in whilst boiling; when cool, put in dry yeast.

YEAST.
Miss Nancy White.

1 quart of mashed potatoes; 1 pint of hops; 1 teacup of molasses; 1 teacup of sugar; 1 teacup of salt; 3 tablespoonfuls of ginger; 1 quart of flour; stir in a gallon of water with the above, and when cool put in 1 pint of "bakers' yeast;" let it ferment; then put it in a cool place.

BREAD.

BREAD.

To test flour, take a handful, press it tight; if it retains its form, it is good; if, on loosening the fingers, it falls to pieces, it is adulterated.

Keep the sponge moderately warm while rising.

If the oven is too cold, the bread will be heavy.

If not well kneaded, it will rise full of large holes.

Good yeast, good flour, good heat and experience, make good bread. Here we find that practice makes perfect. An ounce of practice is worth a pound of theory.

ROLLS.

1 quart of flour; butter or lard the size of an egg; 1 teacup of yeast; a little salt; warm water enough to make a dough; knead together at night; in the morning knead again and make into rolls and put in the pans, and stand until light; then bake.

Graham rolls may be made in the same way, adding one tablespoonful of sugar.

SOFT RAISED ROLLS.
Mrs. H. A. Towne.

1½ cups of sweet milk; 1 egg; butter, size of 2 eggs; ½ teacup of good yeast; 1 tablespoonful of white sugar; salt; mix in flour enough to make a soft dough; beat with a spoon; raise over night; roll out in the morning with as little flour as possible, and cut and raise again before baking.

TEA CAKE (OR RATHER BREAD.)
Mrs. J. W. Collins.

Rub into a quart of dried flour a quarter-pound butter; beat up 2 eggs with 2 teaspoonfuls of sifted sugar and 2 tablespoonfuls of brewers' yeast; pour this liquid mixture in the centre of the flour and add a pint of warm milk; as you mix it, beat it with the hand till it comes off without sticking. Set it to rise before the fire. Let it rise an hour, then make it in cakes an inch thick; set them in tin plates before the fire ten minutes, then bake in a moderate oven. These cakes may be split and buttered hot from the oven, or split, toasted and buttered after they are cold.

MILK TOAST.

Boil a quart of milk, and stir into it three ounces of butter mixed with a tablespoonful of sifted flour and 1 saltspoonful of salt; let it boil five minutes; have a few slices of toasted bread; pour the milk over and send to the table hot.

POCKET BOOKS.
Mrs. H. A. Towne.

1 pint of sponge to 3 pints of flour; 2 eggs; 1 spoonful of lard; if too light, work it down an hour before baking—less time in hot weather; roll the dough out, and sprinkle over it a tablespoonful of loaf sugar and one teaspoonful of soda dissolved in a little warm water; work thoroughly, roll thin and butter the surface; cut with a large biscuit-cutter, turn the buttered edges together, and let it raise again. (A lump of dough that will fill a quart bowl will do to commence on.)

MILK RISING BREAD.

Take one cup of milk, one of water, a teaspoon of salt, and flour to make a batter; keep it warm until light, then warm milk, and mix the rising and milk with sufficient flour to make a soft dough; knead it thoroughly; put into the pans, and bake as soon as light.

NEW ENGLAND MIXED BREAD.
Mrs. H. A. Towne.

1 quart of corn meal; pour boiling water over it till it is well scalded; when cool enough to bear your hand in it, put in half cup of molasses, and a half-pint of yeast (or less will do if very strong); 2 quarts of brown flour; knead it well; let it rise light and bake it in steady and pretty hot oven four hours; bake slow at first.

BREAD GEMS.

Take some pieces of dry bread; soak them over night in cold water; in the morning trim off the brown crust, squeeze out all the water; pour on milk; add flour enough to make a stiff batter, salt, baking powder; a tablespoonful of melted butter to every pint; beat well, and bake in gem irons.

RUSK.
Mrs. Wm. Van Wagenen.

A batter of 1 pint of milk; $\frac{2}{3}$ of a cup of yeast; 2 tablespoons of sugar; after rising add 2 eggs, 1 teacup of sugar, 6 oz. of butter, $\frac{1}{2}$ teaspoonful saleratus; when baked, swab them over with milk and sugar, setting them in the oven for a minute or two to dry.

TO MAKE BREAD.

Set a sponge over night, with one pound of flour, and three or four tablespoonfuls of yeast, and sufficient tepid water to make it into a moderately thick batter. In the morning sift four or five pounds of flour into a deep pan, to which add the sponge, a little salt, and sufficient water to make a dough; knead it well, and then return it to the pan in which it was mixed, and let it rise; when it is light, turn it out on the moulding-board and knead for five or ten minutes, and make in loaves. Butter your pans, put in the loaves, cover them and set to rise in a moderately warm place, and bake, as soon as light, in a rather quick oven.

HOT CROSS BUNS.

Mrs. James Holden.

3 cups sweet milk; 1 cup yeast; flour for thick batter; set over night; in morning add 1 cup sugar; ½ cup butter; ½ nutmeg; salt; flour to roll; knead well; rise till light (say five hours); roll ½ inch thick; cut into round cakes; when they have stood ½ hour make a cross and bake immediately.

BISCUITS.

BAKING POWDER BISCUITS.

Mrs. Harriet C. Damarin.

1 pint of sweet milk; 3 teaspoonfuls of baking powder; 1 quart of flour; mix flour and baking powder well together, then add one heaping tablespoonful of lard in the flour and powder; rub well together, then add the milk; roll thin and bake in a quick oven.

MUSH BISCUIT.

Mrs. Dunlevy.

2 lbs. flour; ½ pint yeast; 1 pint mush; ¼ lb. lard; milk to mix soft; let rise, then make into rolls. Rise again and bake.

SHORT BISCUIT.

1 pint of sweet milk; 3 pints of flour; 1 cup of butter; 1 teaspoonful of salt; 3 teaspoonfuls of baking powder. Rub the baking powder in the flour well, then add the butter and salt; rub these in thoroughly, and add the milk. Mix as quickly as possible, and bake immediately, in a hot oven. A little more flour *may* be required in rolling out, but the dredge should be as soft as can be handled.

BATH BISCUIT.
Mrs. Jas. Holden.

Rub into 2 lbs. flour, ½ lb. butter, and mix with it 1 pint warm milk, ¼ pint yeast, 4 well beaten eggs, a teaspoon salt; let rise three fourths hour; make into thick cake about the size of a dinner plate. Bake in quick oven.

MARYLAND BISCUITS.
Mrs. Jas. Holden.

½ cup butter; ½ cup lard; 7 cups flour; 1 teaspoon salt; wet with water; knead till smooth.

SHORT CAKE FOR FRUIT.
Mrs. Wm. Moore.

1 cup of sour cream; 3 tablespoonfuls of butter; 1 teaspoonful of soda; 3 large cups of flour; rub the butter and flour together well, then add the soda, after powdering it as fine as possible with a knife. When all is ready, add the cream, and mix as quickly as possible. This will make two medium size, to bake in pie pans, or can be baked in one cake in a dripping pan. Split the cake open as soon as it has cooled sufficiently, and put in a thick layer of fruit and sugar.

SODA BISCUIT.

1 qt. of flour; 2 tablespoonfuls of lard, rubbed in the same as pie crust; 2 teacups of sweet milk; 2 teaspoonfuls cream tartar; one-third as much soda; a little salt; mix and roll out, working it as little as possible.

TEA BISCUIT.

1 pint of sweet milk; 4 tablespoons of butter, or lard; 1 tea cup of yeast; the whites of two eggs; yolk of one; 1 tablespoon of white sugar.

Corn Batter Cakes.

CORN JOHNNY CAKE.
Mrs. M. J. Waller.

1 cup of flour; 3 cups corn meal; 1 cup molasses; 2 cups of milk; 3 teaspoons baking powder; 1 teaspoon salt; bake immediately.

RICE PONE.
Mrs. Powell.

Beat 2 eggs very light; 1 cup of rice boiled; piece of butter about the size of an egg; put in the rice, while hot, $\frac{1}{2}$ pint sweet milk, $\frac{1}{2}$ pint Indian meal; stir well together, and bake about half an hour.

CORN BATTER CAKES.
Mrs. Wm. Moore.

1 pint of sour milk; 4 eggs; 1 teaspoonful of soda; 1 tablespoonful of lard; 1 teaspoonful of salt; 1 small cup of flour; corn meal, to make the batter just thick enough to bake; separate the eggs and beat well; add the whites just before baking; they may be made without the flour, but adding the flour gives them a more velvety appearance.

JOHNNY CAKE.
Mrs. Wm. Van Wagenen.

2 cups of Indian meal; 1 cup of flour; 2 eggs; $\frac{3}{4}$ cup of cream; 2 tablespoonfuls of molasses; milk to make it quite thin; 1 teaspoonful saleratus.

CORN BREAD.
Mrs. E. B. Moore.

1 qt. corn meal; 1 qt. of water; ¼ lb of butter; 2 tablespoonfuls sugar; 6 eggs, and salt; 4 teaspoonfuls baking powder in 2 tablespoonfuls flour; pour 1 pt. boiling water over corn meal, other pint cold.

VIRGINIA CORN BREAD.

Melt a tablespoonful of butter, or lard, into 1½ pints of hot milk; into this, stir a pint of meal; when cool, add ¼ of a pint of flour, a tablespoonful of sugar, salt, and 3 beaten eggs; mix well, and bake in pans.

CORN BREAD.
Mrs. C. S. Green.

1 pint of sour milk; 1 pint of sweet milk; one cup of syrup; 1 teaspoonful of soda; 1 tablespoonful of salt; 1½ pints of corn meal; 1 pint of flour; bake three hours in a slow oven.

CORN BREAD.

1 qt. sour milk; 3 eggs; 1 tablespoon butter; 2 even teaspoons soda; salt; mix to a batter, that will run off the spoon, with corn meal; bake, in pie-pans, about 1 inch thick; or the same amount of sweet milk with 3 teaspoons baking powder.

This bread is nice baked in small tin moulds; also, made thinner to fry as griddle cakes.

SWEET CORN BREAD.
Mrs. H. A. Towne.

2 teacups of corn meal; 1 teaspoonful of salt; 2 teacups of white flour; 1 teaspoonful of soda; 1 teacup of molasses; ½ teaspoonful of cream tartar; a piece of butter or lard size of a walnut; about a pint of sweet milk (or water) to mix very thin; stir the salt and cream tartar into the meal, dry, and the soda into the molasses.

 BROWN BREAD.

RYE BREAD.

Set a sponge at night, as for wheat bread, then sift into a deep pan, four pounds of rye flour and one of wheat flour, to which add the sponge and a little salt. Mix with water sufficient to make a moderately soft dough; knead well, and return to the pan in which it was mixed; cover close, and put in a warm place to rise; when light, bake in a quick oven. In cold weather, add a little mush made of corn meal.

BOSTON BROWN BREAD.
Mrs. Syler.

1 pint rye meal; 1 qt. corn meal; 1 egg; 1 cup molasses; 1 quart water; 1 teaspoonful soda; beat well and pour into a tin mould, with a close lid; boil in a kettle of water 4 hours; take out of the mould, and set in a hot oven ten minutes.

BROWN BREAD.
Mrs. H. A. Towne.

2 qts. brown flour, (not sifted;) 1 teacup sugar; 1 teacup yeast; salt; warm water sufficient to mix as stiff as pound cake. Bake hour and half, slowly at first.

BOSTON BREAD.

3 cups corn meal; 1½ cups flour; 1 cup molasses; 1 qt. warm water; 1 tablespoonful vinegar; add soda and salt. Boil four hours. Bake two hours.

GRAHAM BREAD.
Mrs. E. B. Moore.

2 qts. sifted Graham flour; 1 teaspoonful of soda; 1 teaspoonful of yeast; 1 large teaspoonful of salt; mix the above together with a spoon, pretty stiff, melting it up with warm water. Let it rise about three hours, in a cool place; then add one coffeecup of New Orleans molasses, and let it rise about an hour more, and bake about 1½ hours in a quick oven.

BROWN BREAD CAKES.
Mrs. E. R. Merrell.

One pint of sour milk; one teaspoonful of soda; one tablespoon of molasses or sugar; one tablespoon of melted lard; one egg separated, the white beaten; one quart of unbolted flour. Bake half an hour.

GRAHAM BREAD.
Mrs. Wm. Van Wagenen.

1 qt. of unbolted flour; ½ teacup of molasses; a piece of butter about half as large as a hen's egg; stir it up with sweet milk, and one small teaspoonful of soda, making it about the consistency of pound cake.

BROWN BREAD.

Three quarts brown flour, sifted closely; one cup good yeast; one cup molasses, with one teaspoonful soda well beaten into it; mix into a soft sponge with warm water, at night; let rise till morning; then mix into a soft dough; let rise again and work into loaves; let rise again and bake.

STEAMED BOSTON BREAD.
Mrs. H. A. Towne.

2 teacups brown flour; 1 teacup white flour; 1 teacup corn meal; 1 qt. of sweet or sour milk. If sweet milk, 2 teaspoonfuls of cream tartar, and one teaspoonful soda—if sour, only soda.— Steam three hours.

MUFFINS, &C.

SALLY-LUNN.

1½ lbs flour; 1 pint of milk; 2 tablespoonfuls yeast; 3 well beaten eggs; 2 oz. butter; let it rise two or three hours.

GERMAN PUFFS.

6 eggs to 1 qt. of milk; 6 tablespoonfuls of flour; piece of butter the size of an egg; one teaspoon of soda: beat the white of egg separately.

GERMAN PUFFS.

7 spoonfuls flour; 3 eggs; 1 qt. milk; very little salt; beat flour and eggs together, and then add milk. Bake fifteen minutes in cups.

POP-OVERS.
Mrs. Geo. Johnson.

1 cup of sweet milk; 1 cup of flour; 1 egg and salt, will make one dozen. 2 cups of milk, 2 cups of flour, and 2 eggs, will make two dozen. Beat your eggs separately, and very light, and bake in pop over pans.

PUFFETS.
Mrs. M. E. Draper.

2 eggs; 2 tablespoonfuls sugar; 1 pint sweet milk; 1 quart flour; butter, size of an egg; 2 teaspoonfuls cream tartar; 1 teaspoonful salt; 1 teaspoonful soda. Dissolve the soda in a small portion of milk, add just before baking. Bake in muffin rings.

SNOW FLAKES.

1 quart milk; 6 eggs: ½ cup of butter; 3 pints flour; salt; beat it a great deal. Bake in earthen cups in a hot oven.

SUTHERLAND MUFFINS.

1 pint milk; 1 pint flour; 3 eggs; salt. Bake in small round pans or rings.

MUFFINS.

1 egg; two-thirds cup of milk: 1 heaping cup of flour; 1 teaspoon of yeast powder; beat all together well. This quantity makes 6 muffin rings two-thirds full.

MUFFINS.

2 eggs; 1 qt. sour milk; 2 teaspoons soda; 1 qt. flour; 1 tablespoon of lard.

MUFFINS.

To 1½ lbs of flour, 3 eggs, ¼ lb. of butter or lard, a gill of yeast; break the eggs into the flour; add the butter and yeast; wet up with warm milk; grease muffin rings, fill half full and bake. Put a pan of water over the oven, to keep the muffins from having a stiff crust on top. This must be done in all these light breakfast cakes.

MUFFINS.

Mrs. Towell.

Warm 1 qt. of milk with butter size of two eggs; 6 eggs beaten, and mix with milk, and nearly ½ pint of yeast; add flour as thick as can be stirred; stir in a little soda ½ hour before baking. Made in the morning for supper, or over night for breakfast.

RYE OR GRAHAM MUFFINS.

3 cups of rye; 1 of flour; 2 teaspoonfuls of cream of tartar; 1 of soda; 1 tablespoonful of sugar; 1 egg and 1 pint of milk.— For Graham muffins, the flour may be left out.

FRITTERS.

BATTER CAKES.
Mrs. Wm. Moore.

1 pint of sour milk; 4 eggs; 1 teaspoonful of soda; 1 teaspoonful of salt; stir enough flour in the sour milk to make a stiff batter; then add the beaten yolks, the salt, the soda, a tablespoonful of sugar, after the soda, and lastly the well-beaten whites.

WAFFLES.
Mrs. A. McFarland.

Take 1 quart of sour milk; 1 light teaspoonful of soda, and 1 teaspoonful of salt; 4 eggs, and flour enough to make a tolerably stiff batter, put the salt and soda into the milk and stir until dissolved and the milk is light; then add the yolks of the eggs, and then the flour; beat well, and lastly add the whites, which must be beaten to a stiff froth.

BREAD PANCAKES.
Mrs. A. Pursell.

1 qt. boiling sweet milk; 2 cups stale bread crumbs; ½ cup flour; 5 eggs; 2 teaspoonfuls baking powder (in flour); 1 tablespoonful melted butter; 1 teaspoonful salt; soak the bread in the hot milk fifteen minutes; beat smooth; add the yolks, butter and salt, and finally the whites, whipped stiff.

FRITTERS.

6 eggs; 1 quart sweet milk; 3 teaspoonfuls fresh baking powder; salt; flour enough to make a batter; beat the yolks and whites separately; sift the baking powder into the flour; add the whites last, having them whipped very light; fry in hot lard.

ALICE'S WAFFLES.

1 qt. sour milk; 2 teaspoons soda; 3 eggs; 2 tablespoons corn meal; ½ tablespoon lard; ½ tablespoon butter; 1 cup sweet milk; beat eggs separately, and put flour to make as thick as "pancake" dough.

PIES.

PASTRY.

Handle paste as little as possible; roll it very lightly; don't wet it too much, it makes it tough. Fresh butter is best; wash the salt out, and it will be nicer. Lard does not make so light or so finely flavored a puff paste as butter. Flour both sides before you bake it, this will give the paste a fine color; by folding and rolling several times, it rises higher and more even. Cooks agree in this, that puff paste must always be rolled from you. Put very small lumps of butter over the puff paste after you have rolled it; dredge with flour; fold it over; roll thin; repeat the process as before.

Do not make your paste until you are ready to bake it. Have your oven hot and ready.

If the oven is too hot, paste will not rise well; the same, if it is too cold. Keep your oven swept and clean; never permit juice to run over.

MINCED MEAT.

Four pounds of fresh tongue or beef; Two pounds of suet; eight pounds of chopped apples; three pounds of currants, washed and picked; three pounds of raisins, seeded and cut in halves; six pounds of sugar; two pounds of citron, cut in thin pieces; the rind of one orange, chopped fine; one ounce of cinnamon; a quarter of an ounce of cloves; a quarter of an ounce of mace; a quarter of an ounce of allspice; four nutmegs, grated; 1 quart of the syrup of spiced fruit; one pint of good vinegar; boil the meat in salted water until tender; when cold, chop it fine; also the suet, mixing it with the meat, with salt just sufficient to remove the fresh taste; to this add the apples, then the fruit, sugar, spices and other ingredients. Mix all well together, and cover close. If too dry (before using) add a little water.

MINCE PIES.
Mrs. C. G. Young.

4 pints of meat; 1 lb raisins; 1 lb. currants; 2 pints of suet; ½ pint molasses; salt, pepper, cider; 1 tablespoon cinnamon; ½ tablespoon allspice; nutmegs; sweeten to taste. Two pints of the above mixture, and one of apples.

MOCK MINCE PIE.
Miss. Julia Pursell.

½ cup molasses; 1 cup sugar; 1 cup chopped raisins; ½ cup vinegar; ¼ cup butter; 3 cups boiling water; 3 eggs, (well beaten;) 3 crackers, rolled fine; 1 teaspoon cloves; 2 teaspoonfuls cinnamon; ½ small nutmeg. This quantity makes four pies.

TEMPERANCE MINCE PIE.

To four pounds of meat (beef,) after it is prepared, 3 lbs. of suet, 3 lbs. of raisins, 3 lbs. of currants, 3 lbs. of citron, 3 lbs. of best brown sugar, 1 large spoonful of salt, the juice of twelve lemons, and the rind of six, grated and cut fine, 1 pint of best syrup of molasses, 2 oz. of cinnamon, 1 oz. cloves, 1 oz. of allspice, or nutmeg. Mix these ingredients well together, and pack lightly in a jar (stone,) with a layer of sugar over it, till ready to bake. To one-third of the quantity, add one-half a peck of good pippin apples, chopped fine, the juice of eight lemons and two quarts of water, and one lb. of sugar.

PUMPKIN PIE.

To 1 pint of stewed and strained pumpkin, take 1 qt. of sweet milk, a pinch of salt, and 6 eggs. Ginger, nutmeg or cinnamon are good spices for these pies. Bake in rich paste.

PUMPKIN PIES.

To three cups of the pumpkin strained, add one cup of cream three eggs, a little cinnamon and nutmeg, (some prefer a little ginger;) make it thin with hot milk.

FLOUR PIE.

Stir one teacup of sifted flour in a quart of boiling milk, and yolks of three eggs; let boil a few minutes; sweeten, and add a piece of one lemon; have the crusts baked, and fill with the custard; spread over the tops, the whites which have been well beaten and sweetened, and brown slightly; wet the flour with a little cold milk before stirring in.

PEACH COBBLERS.

Make a light dough of baking powder, and very little shortening; roll thin, and line the sides and ends of a small bread pan; peel the peaches; put them in with enough water to cook them and make plenty of juice; cover on top with a crust, leaving holes on top for the steam to escape; bake until the peaches are quite tender, in a slow oven; lift all the crust; cut into small pieces; spread each piece with peaches and juice; sprinkle sugar and small lumps of butter all over, and eat with cream or milk. Apple cobblers in the same way.

CUSTARD PIE.

3 eggs; 3 tablespoons of sugar; 1 pint of milk; cinnamon or nutmeg, or any flavoring to taste; beat the eggs and sugar until light and spongy; add sugar and flavoring; pour into the crust and bake in a moderate oven. Don't open the oven for twenty minutes.

CHEESE-CAKE.
Mrs. Col. Kinney.

4 qts. of new milk, put rennet in it; when it is well curded, tie it in a cloth and drain the whey from it; put the curd in a hair seive, with 1 lb. of butter, and rub through with a spoon; add the yolks of 12 eggs; 12 spoons of rosewater, or lemon juice; 2 grated nutmegs; sweeten to taste; 1 lb. of currants; mix all together and bake. For the crust take 1 lb. of flour, yolks of three eggs, 6 oz. of sugar, and as much butter as will mix these to a paste.

SAND TARTS.

2 eggs; 2 cups of sugar; 1½ cups of butter; flour enough to roll very stiff; whites of two eggs; 1½ cups of clarified sugar; ½ teaspoonful of lemon; sugar and cinnamon sprinkled over the top; boil the sugar like candy, and pour it over the beaten eggs, then put it on the cakes, with almonds blanched; sugar and cinnamon over the top.

DEDHAM CREAM PIE.
Mrs. C. G. Young.

Make the pie crust not too rich, and bake as for puffs. THE CREAM—1 pint of milk; ½ cup of flour; 1 cup of sugar; yolks of 2 eggs; a little salt; grated rind and juice of 2 lemons; put on the stove, and cook to a thick custard; fill the crust with the cream; then take ½ cup of sugar to the whites of three eggs, and make an icing; spread over the top of the pie, put in the oven and brown.

PUFF PASTE.

2 lbs. flour; 1 lb. butter; put a little butter in, and make it light with cold water, just stiff enough to work up, then roll it thin and put a layer of butter all over; sprinkle on a little flour, double it up and roll it out again; double it and roll three times.

PIE-PLANT PIE.

One pint of stewed pie-plant rubbed through a cullender; one-half pint of cream; one-half pint of sugar; one teacup of rolled crackers; three eggs; mix all together, and bake without an upper crust.

COCOANUT PIE.
Mrs. A. P.

1 quart of sweet milk (let this come to a boil); 1 grated cocoanut; 2 heaping tablespoonfuls corn starch; 4 eggs; enough sugar to sweeten; bake in puff paste.

KENTUCKY PIE.
Mrs. J. W. Collins.

2 coffee cups sugar; ¾ coffee cup butter; 1 coffee cup cream; 3 tablespoonfuls flour; season with nutmeg or lemon; bake in a crust as you would custard pie.

PASTRY.

1 cup of lard; 3 cups of flour; 1 cup of water; a little salt; mix lightly, roll out, and spread on it bits of butter; sprinkle on a little flour, roll again, repeat twice; enough for two pies.

LEMON PIE.
Miss Kate Glover.

2 lemons; 1½ cups sugar; 4 eggs; 1½ cups of hot water; 6 tablespoons flour; butter size of a walnut; grate the pulp of

the lemons and a portion of the rind also; beat the sugar and yolks of eggs well, and add to the lemon; then the flour, the water, almost boiling, and the butter; for the icing, take 5 tablespoons of sugar to the whites of the eggs, first beating the eggs well; after the pies are baked, spread on the icing, and let them remain in the oven until a light brown.

LEMON PIE (A VERY RICH PIE).
Mrs. E. B. Moore.

3 eggs; 3 lemons; 3 sponge cakes (small square ones); 2 cups of sugar; ½ cup of water; beat the yolks of eggs and sugar together till very light; then add the lemon juice and grated sponge cakes; then the water; just before filling in the paste, add the grated rind of the lemons and the whites of the eggs, beaten to a stiff froth. (This makes two full pies.)

LEMON PIE.
Mrs. Hull.

2 lemons; 2 cups of sugar; 3 tablespoonfuls of corn starch; 2 large cups of boiling water poured on the corn starch (having previously wet the same with cold water); a small piece of butter in the starch while hot; 2 eggs; when cool, mix all together and bake with an under crust.

LEMON PUFFS.
Mrs. Mary S. Ingalls.

1 ℔ of sugar; ½ ℔ of butter; 5 eggs, leaving out the whites of 3; the juice of 2 lemons, and the rind of 1 cut very fine; mix the ingredients, and put it on the fire; let it simmer until it becomes thick as honey, then remove it from the fire; when cool, bake in a rich paste; beat the three whites with three tablespoonfuls of white sugar to a cream, and spread on top; let it remain in the oven to brown slightly.

LEMON PIE.
Mrs. W. A. Hutchins.

To juice and rind of one lemon, add 1 cup of sugar, the yolks of 3 eggs, 1 teaspoonful of butter, and sufficient milk to fill the pan; bake in rich paste; beat the whites to stiff froth, add sugar, and spread over the pie after it is baked; brown slightly.

LEMON PIE.
Mrs. Mary E. Draper.

1 quart of milk; 8 eggs (beaten separately); 3 lemons; ¼ lb of butter; ¼ lb of flour; rub well together the butter and flour; scald the milk and pour over the butter and flour, allowing it to stand until cold; add to the yolks of the eggs the grated rind of one lemon and the juice of 3; sweeten to your taste; bake with an undercrust; when nearly done, take from the oven and spread the whites of the eggs on the top, with which has been beaten a little pulverized sugar; return to the oven to brown.

LEMON PIE.
Miss Katie Johnson, Steubenville, Ohio.

Grate one lemon to one cup of hot water, two cups of sugar, the yolks of four eggs, a lump of butter as large as a walnut, four tablespoonfuls of flour, stirred smooth in cold water; line two pans with crust, divide this into them, and bake; beat the whites of the four eggs to a stiff froth; add four tablespoonfuls sugar; spread on when the pies are baked; put in the oven, and slightly brown.

PERPETUAL LEMON CHEESE CAKE.
Miss E. Bell.

1 lb of loaf sugar; 6 eggs, leaving out two whites; the juice of 3 fine lemons, and grated rind of 2; ¼ lb of fresh butter; put all in a pan and boil gently until they are as thick as honey; pour in a small jar covered air tight; a dessert spoonful is sufficient for each puff.

CREAM PIES.
Mrs. J. W. Collins.

3 eggs; 1 cup of sugar; butter size of a walnut; 1 teaspoonful of cream tartar; ½ teaspoonful of soda; coffee cup of flour,

all mixed well together; bake in two pans; when perfectly cold, put between the following: Put on to boil 1 pint of milk; take 4 eggs, 1 teacup of sugar and a large spoonful of flour mixed well, and pour in the milk while boiling; when this is cold, flavor with vanilla, and it is ready to put between the cakes; eat as other pies; remember to split each cake, for this quantity makes two pies.

CREAM PIE.
Mrs. E. B. Moore.

2 tablespoonfuls of flour; 2 tablespoonfuls of sugar; 1 pint of cream; a little nutmeg; bake in a crust.

CREAM PIE.
Mrs. H. A. Towne.

1 pt. of good sweet cream; 2 tablespoonfuls flour mixed with 4 tablespoonfuls of white sugar pulverized, 2 eggs; use only the whites, beaten stiff, vanilla, add sugar to taste, if not already sweet enough; mix in the whites of eggs last, after the other ingredients; bake without an upper crust.

PUDDINGS

Beef suet is best, mutton next.

Soak rice a half an hour before using.

Stone raisins, cutting them once with a knife is nicer than chopping.

Wash currants; pour boiling water on to make them swell; dry before the fire.

Puddings may be boiled in a form or bag; rub the form with suet or butter; dip the bag in boiling water, and flour the inside. Tie batter puddings tight.

Tie bread or corn meal puddings loose.

Let the water boil before you put them in.

Have water enough to cover and turn the bag often; don't let the water come quite to the top of the form or tin.

As soon as done, give whatever it is boiled in a sudden plunge in cold water. Turn out quickly, and serve as soon as turned out.

For custards, bread pudding, corn meal, &c., have a moderate oven.

Batter, a quick oven.

TAPIOCA PUDDING.
Mrs H. L. Miller.

4 tablespoonfuls of tapioca; 1 qt. of milk; 5 eggs; 4 tablespoonfuls of sugar; 1 tablespoonful of butter; a little salt; soak the tapioca in sufficient water to cover it, two hours, then to this

add the butter, sugar, and yolks of the eggs, well beaten together, and put in the oven and bake an hour. Beat the whites thoroughly, taking half and stirring in the hot pudding, then beat up a little sugar with the other half of the whites and spread over the top and set in the oven for a few minutes.

LEMON SAUCE FOR PUDDING.
Mrs. H. L. Miller.

1 coffeecup of sugar; ½ coffeecup of butter; 1 egg; 1 lemon, juice and grated rind; 1 teaspoonful of nutmeg; 4 tablespoons of boiling water; cream the butter and sugar and beat in the eggs; add the lemon and nutmeg; beat hard ten minutes, and add, a spoonful at a time of the boiling water. Put in a tin basin and set in the uncovered top of the tea kettle, which must be kept boiling, until the steam heats the sauce very hot; stir constantly.

SOUFLE PUDDING.
Mrs. H. A. Towne.

Boil ¾ cup of butter in a sauce pan, with 3 tablespoonfuls of flour, stirring all the time; add 1 tumblerful of sweet milk, and stir till it is of the consistency of starch; take from the fire and add quickly the unbeaten yolks of four eggs. Just before dinner, add the whites of the eggs beaten, and two tablespoonfuls of white sugar. Flavor to taste, and bake twenty minutes. Eaten with a sauce.

COTTAGE PUDDING.

1 cup of sugar; 1 cup of sweet milk; 3 cups of flour; ½ cup of butter; 2 small teaspoonfuls of baking powder; 3 eggs, whites beaten. Bake ½ an hour.

ORANGE PUDDING.
Mrs. Dickinson.

½ lb. of butter; ½ lb. of white sugar; 1 cup of cream; 6 eggs; 2 oranges, juice and rind; 1 tablespoon of grated cracker; beat butter and sugar together, the eggs separately; stir into the but-

ter and sugar; add cream and cracker; bake in a flat dish.—
When done, beat the whites of three eggs with 2 spoonfuls of
sugar, spread over, and bake a light brown.

TAYLOR PUDDING.
Mrs. H. A. Towne.

1 cup of milk; 1 cup of suet, chopped; 1 cup of molasses; 2
cups of fruit; 4 cups of flour; 2 teaspoonfuls of soda. Boil four
or five hours.

PUDDING.
Mrs. Dickinson.

1 lb. of sponge cake sliced up in a pudding dish; boil 1 qt. of
milk; thicken with 1 dessert spoonful of arrow root, or corn
starch; flavor with stick of cinnamon, or any flavor; when it
boils, add the yolk of five eggs, pour it on the cake; bake in the
stove a few minutes; mix the white of eggs, well beaten, with 4
spoonfuls of sugar; spread over the top of pudding, and set in the
oven until brown.

JELLY PUDDING.
Mrs. J. W. Clarke.

Put slices of jelly cake in the dish, with a small piece of butter; sprinkle each layer with mace, until the dish is filled, then
beat the yolks of two eggs with 1 cup of milk, 1 tablespoon of
sugar, and pour over the top; when baked, beat the two whites
with 4 tablespoonfuls of sugar; spread jelly over the top, and
then add the whites and sugar, and let it stand in the oven until
it crisps on the top.

SNOW PUDDING.

Pour one pint of boiling water on half a box of gelatine; add
juice of one lemon, and two cups of sugar; when nearly cold,
strain it; add the whites of 3 eggs, beaten to a stiff froth, then
beat all well together again; put it into a mould to shape it,

and let it cool; take the yolks of these eggs, one pint of milk and teaspoon of corn starch; flavor with vanilla. Cook this like any soft custard. Put the hard part of the pudding into a dish when you want to serve it, with the custard around it.

CITRON PUDDING.
Mrs. Dickinson.

Line a pie plate with paste; put in 2 layers of sliced citron; beat well ¾ lb sugar, ¾ lb butter, 10 eggs, leaving out the whites, pour it on the top of the citron and bake.

SUNDERLAND PUDDING.
Mrs. Mary E. Draper.

Six eggs; three tablespoonfuls of flour; one pint of milk; salt; beat the yolks well, and mix them smoothly with the flour; add the milk and salt, and lastly beat the whites to a stiff froth, and work in immediately. Requires one-half hour for baking. To be eaten with "hard sauce," made of butter and pulverized sugar.

TAPIOCA PUDDING.
Mrs. A. McFarland.

Put a teacup of tapioca in a pint and a half of cold water over night; in the course of the morning, peel half a dozen sour apples and steam until tender; put them in a pudding dish; add a teacup and a half of sugar, a little salt and a teacupful of water to the tapioca, and pour over the apples; slice a lemon thin and lay over the top of the pudding. Bake slowly, two hours. Serve with cream.

HUNTINGTON PUDDING, (EXCELLENT.)
Mrs. Dickinson.

Boil a teacup of washed rice in a quart of milk; when done, add the yolks of four well beaten eggs, a little salt and a tablespoonful of butter; add the grated rind of a lemon and a teacup of sugar. Put in a baking dish. When done, spread the whites on the top, after they have been beaten, with 6 spoonfuls of sugar, and the juice of the lemon added; put back in the stove to brown the meringue.

CUSTARD PUDDING.
Mrs. Wm. Van Wagenen.

1 qt. of milk; 4 eggs; sweeten to your taste; after beating the eggs, pour in the milk with raisins, or other fruit, then spread slices of bread and butter, placing them upon the top, which form a nice crust. To be eaten with sauce unless you make it sufficiently sweet, add nutmeg.

CORN STARCH PUDDING.
Mrs. Wm. Van Wagenen.

1 qt. of milk; 2 tablespoonfuls of corn starch; 5 of sugar; the yolks of 4 eggs; stir and boil together thoroughly; then whip the whites to a froth with sugar, cover it and put it into the oven until a light brown.

SUET PUDDING.
Mrs. Wm. Van Wagenen.

1 cup of suet, chopped fine; 1 egg, beaten; 1 cup of molasses; $\frac{1}{2}$ cup of sugar; 1 slice of bread, crumbled fine; $\frac{1}{2}$ cup of sour milk; 1 cup of raisins; $\frac{1}{2}$ cup of currants; 1 teaspoonful of soda; a little salt; thicken with flour, and steam it three hours. Eat with sauce.

LEMON BUTTER.
Mrs. Kate Wait.

Two lemons; one pint of sugar; one-half cup of butter; three eggs; beat the butter and sugar to a cream; add the eggs, well beaten, then the juice and grated rind of lemons. Put in a tin vessel, and boil in a kettle of water until it thickens.

PLUM PUDDING.
Mrs. A. L. Ratcliff.

1 lb seeded raisins; 1 lb currants; 1 lb suet, chopped very fine; 2 tablespoons cut citron; 1 teaspoonful ground ginger; 1 tea-

spoonful allspice; 1 nutmeg; 4 eggs; 1 small teacup full of molasses; 2 lbs flour, and a little light bread; mix with sweet milk; boil steadily 4 hours. Sauce of drawn butter and sugar, flavored to suit the taste.

REVERE HOUSE PUDDING.
Mrs. Mary E. Draper.

1 cup of chopped suet; 1 cup of sweet milk; 1 cup of molasses; 3 cups of flour; 1 cup of chopped raisins; salt; 1 teaspoon saleratus; cloves, cinnamon and allspice. Grease a tin bucket and boil 3 hours.

DANDY PUDDING.

One quart of milk, boiled by placing the vessel in water; mix two tablespoons of corn starch with the yolk of four eggs, and a half cup of sugar; pour into the milk and stir quickly, and bake at once; beat the whites of the eggs well with a cup of sugar; spread over the pudding when cool. Brown in the oven, and flavor to taste. Eat cold.

FIG PUDDING.

½ lb of figs; ½ cup of suet; ½ lb bread crumbs; 1 tablespoon of sugar; 3 eggs; 1 cup of milk; chop the suet and figs fine; flavor with cinnamon or nutmeg; boil three hours. Eat with sauce.

DELMONICO PUDDING.
Mrs. Geo. Johnson.

1 qt. sweet milk; 3 eggs; 3 tablespoonfuls of corn starch; 1 cup of sugar; flavor with lemon, or anything to your taste; boil the milk and thicken it with corn starch, then add the yolks of eggs; beat the whites separate, and put on top, and set it in the oven to brown. Eat when cold, with jelly.

SWEET POTATO PUDDING.
Mrs. J. W. Collins.

2 large sweet potatoes, grated; 1 qt. of milk; 1 teaspoon of

ginger; 2 tablespoons of sugar; 4 tablespoons of butter; 4 eggs; ½ cup of flour; beat eggs separately; nutmeg. Eat with jelly or cream.

KISS PUDDING.
Miss E. Bell.

Boil one quart of milk. Take three tablespoons of fine starch, yolks of four eggs, ½ cup of sugar, beat together and stir in milk; stir a few moments after it boils, and pour into a deep dish; beat the whites of four eggs; 1 teacup of pulverized sugar; 3 teaspoons of vanilla; juice of 1 lemon; pour on top of pudding. Bake fifteen minutes. Serve cold.

SAUCE FOR PUDDING.

1 cup of sugar; ½ tablespoon of butter; 1 heaping tablespoon of flour; 1 teaspoon of ground cinnamon, or any spice preferred, stir it well together, and pour on 1 qt. of boiling water; stir it until it boils, and add 2 small tablespoons of vinegar. The vinegar may be omitted.

PUDDING.

Put a qt. of milk to boil, when boiled, pour it over a pint of bread crumbs, grated; beat the yolks of four eggs; 1 cup of white sugar; ¼ cup of butter, melted; the grated rind of a lemon. Bake it, and eat cold.

SAUCE FOR PUDDING.
Mrs. Powell.

Cream together ½ lb of butter, ½ lb of brown sugar; break an egg and stir in the yolk; add 1 gill of vinegar. Stir all together well, over some embers, until it thickens.

DRIED CHERRY PUDDING.
Mrs. Powell.

Beat 4 eggs very light; add 1 cup of white sugar; ½ pint of sweet milk; 6 oz. of flour, and 8 oz. of grated bread; 12 ounces of chopped suet, and a little salt; when well beaten, mix in 16 or 18 ounces of cherries; turn frequently while boiling, to prevent fruit from settling. Boil from three to four hours.

PLUM PUDDING.

Three cups of flour; 1 cup of molasses; one cup of milk; one cup of raisins; one cup of suet; one teaspoon of soda; teaspoon of salt. Spice to taste.

BREAD PLUM PUDDING.
Miss Alice L. Ross.

½ lb of fresh bread, cut in small pieces; ½ lb of raisins; ½ lb of suet; ½ lb of currants; ¼ lb of citron; ½ lb of sugar and 6 eggs. Nutmeg and cinnamon to taste, and boil in a bag half an hour. Serve with egg sauce.

QUEEN'S BREAD PUDDING.
Mrs. J. W. Clarke.

1 pint of bread crumbs to 1 quart of milk; four eggs, two whites reserved; half cup of sugar; a piece of butter the size of an egg; a little nutmeg. After the pudding is baked, spread over the top, currant jelly, or preserves of small fruit. Beat the two whites with two tablespoonfuls sugar, and spread over the top. Sauce of sugar and butter beaten stiff, or sweetened cream.

TRANSPARENT PUDDING.
Mrs. J. W. Collins.

1 cup of sugar beaten with three eggs; 1 cup of butter washed free from salt; grated peel of a lemon; line your pie dish with pastry; pour in part of the custard; cover with slices of jelly, then cover with the remaining custard.

BAKED INDIAN PUDDING.
Mrs. H. A.

Boil one pint of milk, stir in one cup of sifted meal while boiling; remove from the fire and add one-half cup of molasses, two tablespoonfuls of sugar, one-half teaspoonful of salt, one teaspoonful of ginger, a little nutmeg, one pint of cold milk, and one egg well beaten; pour into the baking dish while warm, and bake one hour. We use cream and sugar for sauce with this, but it is very nice without any sauce.

BREAD AND BUTTER PUDDING.
S. E. F.

Cover the bottom of a dish with thin slices of bread and butter, then a layer of currants, and so on until the dish is full. Make a custard and pour over it. Let it stand to soak, then bake.

SUET PUDDING.

1 coffeecup of chopped suet; 2 teacups of sugar; 1 teacup of sour milk; 1 teacup of raisins, chopped fine: 3 eggs; 2 teaspoonfuls of baking powder; add flour to make the consistency of fruit cake; flavor with nutmeg. Sauce of sugar, butter and one egg, beaten very light.

CRACKER PUDDING.

6 crackers, pounded fine; 1 qt. of boiling milk; 1 spoonful of flour; 1 cup of brown sugar; 6 eggs; raisins, currants and spices—bake. Very nice.

STARCH PUDDING.

To 1 quart of sweet milk 4 eggs, well beaten; 1 cup of starch; mix with milk; add the eggs and starch when the milk comes to a boil. Let it cook until it thickens, then pour in moulds.— Serve with sugar and cream.

BAKED INDIAN PUDDING.

Scald one pint of sweet milk (do not let it boil;) take a half pint of corn meal, moisten it with cold milk and stir in the scalding milk; take one egg, beat well with sugar, and one-fourth pint of milk to the egg and sugar, and then stir into the pudding; spice it, and add a piece of butter the size of an egg. Bake one hour.

STEAM PUDDING.
Mrs. Syler.

1 cup of butter, or suet; 1 cup of sugar; 2 cups of flour; 2 eggs; ½ cup of water; one teaspoonful of baking powder; 1 cup of currants; steam 2 hours. Sauce to suit taste.

APPLE PUDDING.

For appple pudding, take bread crumbs, suet, apples, currants, and brown sugar, half a pound of each; a dozen of sweet almonds, chopped fine; a little cinnamon and spice to taste. The apples to be pared, cored and chopped. Mix all well together, adding the whites of eggs, which should be the last ingredient put in. Boil for three hours, either in a pudding bag or a mould, well buttered.

CREAM BATTER PUDDING.

Take half a pint of sour cream, half a pint of sweet milk, half pint of flour, three eggs, a little salt, one-half of a teaspoonful of soda; beat the eggs separate, adding the whites last. Bake two and a half hours. The above is the queen of puddings.

POOR MAN'S PUDDING.

One pint of sour milk, one teaspoonful soda, one egg, salt; stir as thick as pound cake, add fruit of any kind, and boil an hour and a half, or steam two hours.

POOR MAN'S PUDDING.
Mrs. M. J. Waller.

1 qt. milk; 6 eggs; 6 tablespoons of flour and a little salt. Bake half hour; use butter and sugar dip.

APPLE DUMPLINGS.

Pare, quarter and core some tart apples and half fill a three pint dish, and nearly cover them with water. Make a crust of one pint of flour, one teaspoonful of cream of tartar, one-half teaspoonful of soda, one cup of milk; roll out and cover the apples, place it on top of the stove, and put another dish the same size over it, and let it steam and cook half an hour. For sauce take two large spoonfuls of butter mixed with one spoonful of flour, add one pint of boiling water, stir quickly and let it boil; add two-thirds cup of sugar, half a nutmeg, a little salt, and let it boil. Try it, and you will make more.

CRACKER DESSERT.

I do not remember to have seen in print directions for making a quick, and cheap, and pretty, and palatable dessert, which I learned how to make many years ago. Choose whole soda crackers, and lay each one upon a separate small plate. Pour upon it enough boiling water to soak it well, and leave none upon the plate; cover with a dressing of good sweetened cream with a spoonful of jelly in the centre if you choose, or dip upon it a portion of nice fruit, canned, stewed or fresh, as is convenient.

APPLE, CURRANT OR DAMSON DUMPLINGS OR PUDDINGS.

Make a paste of suet, or sweet dripping, and line a basin with it, tolerably thin; fill with the fruit and cover it; tie a cloth tight over it, and boil till the fruit shall be done enough.

COCOANUT CUSTARD.

1 lb grated cocoanut; 1 pint of milk; 6 oz. of sugar; yolks of 6 eggs, well beaten; stir into the milk alternately with the cocoanut and sugar; place it in a vessel of boiling water, and stir until thick and smooth. As soon as it comes to a hard boil, take it off, and serve in cups or tumblers.

TAPIOCA CUSTARD.
Mrs. A. Buskirk.

A small teacup of tapioca put to soak over night in a pint of milk; in the morning, add to this 4 tablespoons of sugar, and the yolks of four eggs, then stir this in a quart of milk, boiling; let it cook as float; when wanted for the table, beat up the white and stir in the custard. Flavor to taste.

BAKED CUSTARD.
Mrs. E. Glover.

3 eggs; 1 pint of milk; sugar to taste, flavoring. Let the milk boil; beat the yolks of eggs and sugar until very light; stir them into the boiling milk; do not stop stirring until it boils again, and then take it off the fire immediately; pour it in a shallow dish; beat the white of eggs very light; spread over the top and bake in the oven until a light brown, which will be done in about five to ten minutes.

CHOCOLATE CREAM CUSTARD.
Mrs. M. J. Waller.

Scrape $\frac{1}{4}$ lb of chocolate; pour on it a teacup of boiling water; let it stand by the fire until dissolved; beat 8 eggs lightly, omitting the whites of two; stir them by degrees into a qt. of rich cream, alternately with the chocolate and 3 tablespoons of white sugar; put in dish and bake 10 minutes.

APPLE CUSTARD.

1 pint of stewed and strained apples; $\frac{1}{4}$ lb of butter; $\frac{1}{2}$ pint of cream; 3 eggs, beaten light; sugar and nutmeg to taste; mix the ingredients and bake in puff paste, in a moderate oven.

FLUMMERY.
Mrs. C. S. Smith.

The whites of two eggs; 1 teacup of white sugar; $\frac{1}{2}$ tumbler of jelly, of any kind; beat all together until very stiff. Jelly, a little acid is best.

COCOANUT BLANC MANGE.

Boil 1 qt. of milk, stir in 1 grated cocoanut, 3 tablespoonfuls of corn starch; add milk to soften it, and enough sugar to sweeten it, and a little salt; let it cook 20 minutes, stirring occasionally, then remove from oven, and stir in lightly, the beaten whites of 4 eggs; pour in a mould, and when cold, serve with sugar and cream.

BAKED CUSTARD.

1 pint of milk, good measure; 3 eggs; 1 tablespoonful of sugar: beat the eggs and sugar until very light, then add the milk and stir well. Bake in a quick oven; try it often with a spoon, to see whether it is solid, and just at that moment, remove it from the oven; baked too long, it gets watery.

CHARLOTTE RUSSE.
Mrs. H. A. Towne.

3 eggs, well beaten; 6 oz. of sugar in ½ pint of milk, flavored with vanilla, boiled; 1 oz. of gelatine dissolved in ½ pint of milk; stir the gelatine into the custard; when perfectly cool, add 1 qt. of whipped cream. Put into mould lined with sponge cake.

CHARLOTTE RUSSE.
Mrs. A. W. Buskirk.

2 oz. of Russia isinglass in 1 qt. of fresh milk; let it soak three hours; beat the yolks of 8 eggs and 1 lb of sugar very thoroughly together; boil the isinglass and milk, and add the egg and sugar while boiling; stir in two qts. of sweet cream; flavor to taste, and pour in a mould.

APPLE FLOAT.
Miss E. Bell.

To the whites of 6 eggs, well beaten, add 2 teacups of apples, boiled and strained; 1 cup of sugar; beat all together thoroughly. Flavor to taste.

APPLE FLOAT.
Mrs. M. J. Waller.

6 large apples; pare, slice and stew in as much water as will

cover them; when well done, press through a sieve; make very sweet with crushed sugar; beat the whites of 4 eggs to a froth; stir in the apples when cool; flavor with lemon or vanilla. Serve with cream.

FLOAT.
Mrs. Wm. Moore.

1 qt. of sweet milk; 5 eggs; 2 tablespoonfuls of sugar; flavoring extract to suit the taste; put the milk in a vessel and place this in another, containing boiling water; when the milk is almost boiling, add the beaten yolks, putting in a little at a time, and stirring briskly; let this cook until of the right consistency, then stir in the whites, which must also be well beaten. After the float has been removed from the vessel in which it was cooked, add the flavoring.

Sauce for Puddings.

CREAM SAUCE.

1 cup of sweet, fresh butter; 2½ cups of white sugar; 1 egg; beat these together until it becomes a white and very light cream; flavor with lemon or vanilla.

COLD SAUCE FOR PUDDINGS OR APPLE DUMPLINGS.

Take 4 large spoonfuls of fine white sugar, and 2 of butter stir to a cream, and flavor with lemon or vanilla, or grate nutmeg on the top if you prefer.

ELEGANT PUDDING SAUCE.
From Mrs. Cornelius' Cook Book.

To 4 spoonfuls of fine white sugar, put 2 of butter, 1 of flour, and stir them together to a cream in an earthen dish; cut the white of an egg to a stiff froth, and add it; then pour into the dish a gill of boiling water, stirring the mixture very fast; put it into the sauce tureen and add essence of lemon or rose, or grate nutmeg over the top, as you prefer.

Custards, Creams, etc.

WHIPPED CREAM.
Mrs. Wm. Van Wagenen.

Whip 1 pint of sweet cream to a stiff froth; add sugar or lemon, vanilla, and a sheet of isinglass or gelatine, after soaking it.

GELATINE.
Mrs. W. A. Hutchins.

Pour over 3 sliced lemons 1 pint boiling water; add tablespoonful ground cinnamon; let stand until cold, strain, and pour over 1 box Cox's gelatine; when dissolved, add three pints of boiling water, and sugar to taste; strain, and set away to cool.

LEMON CREAM.

The juice and grated peel of one lemon; rub smooth 2 table spoonfuls of corn starch in the yolks of three eggs, 1 cup of sugar and 1 pint of boiling water; when done, beat the 3 whites and stir them in; then pour it into small glasses or cups and set them in the refrigerator on ice to get very cold.

RASPBERRY CREAM.
Mrs. Powell.

Put some raspberries or jam through a hair sieve, to take out the seeds; if the raw fruit, it will require sugar; mix it well with some cream; put it in glasses, and put frothed cream over it; always put a little sugar in the cream as you wish it, and let it remain on the sieve an hour to get firm.

SPANISH CREAM.

½ oz. isinglass or gelatine dissolved in 1 qt. sweet milk; 4 eggs (the yolks); 2 cups of sugar beaten well with the eggs; stir them in the milk till it thickens; set aside to cool; add flavoring and the whites beaten to a stiff froth.

ICE CREAM.

2 gals. rich milk; 16 eggs; 2½ lbs. white pulverized sugar; 4 tablespoons corn starch, beaten with the yolks; beat the whites separately; cook milk, yolks and corn starch, beat in the whites and stir until cold, then add sugar and flavor to suit taste; freeze immediately.

PHILADELPHIA ICE CREAM.

Boil 1 pint of milk and 2 tablespoonfuls of arrow root, and stir until cool, then add two quarts of cream, sweeten and flavor to taste, and freeze.

BAVARIAN CREAM.
Mrs. C. S. Smith.

Soak ½ of a box of gelatine in 1 qt. of milk ½ hour; then add 2 tablespoonfuls of sugar, and 2 eggs; boil all together for a few minutes; when done, add flavoring of any kind you choose, and pour into moulds like jelly; serve cold; with cream it is much better.

ITALIAN CREAM.
Mrs. H. A. Towne.

1 qt. sour milk; 8 eggs, use only the yolks; ½ oz. gelatine or isinglass; sugar to taste, and flavoring; soak in cold water 3 sheets of corpus isinglass 2 hours, or ½ oz. of gelatine; then put it in the milk to boil, stirring it often; when it has dis-

solved and the milk has boiled, stir into it the well-beaten yolks; sweeten, flavor and turn into moulds previously wet with a little white of egg and water; it needs to stand a long time—ten hours at least; needs no straining.

SPANISH CREAM.
Mrs Hull.

Break 1 oz. of isinglass in 3 pints of milk, and put over the fire; beat the yolks of 6 eggs with 6 tablespoonfuls of powdered sugar; beat the whites to a stiff froth; when the isinglass is dissolved and the milk is almost boiling, stir in the yolks; then take it from the fire, stir a few times, and put in the whites of the eggs, flavor with vanilla, and turn into moulds; it is better to be made the day before it is to be eaten, as it should be cool.

ITALIAN CREAM.

1 pt. of cream flavored and sweetened to the taste; 1 oz. of sheet isinglass boiled in 3 cups of water; strain it, cool partially, then add the cream and place in moulds till perfectly cold.

CREAM CHARLOTTE.

Line a dish with lady fingers or sliced sponge cake; 1 qt. of cream, 1 oz. of American isinglass, flour, and sweeten the cream to your taste; whip it to a stiff froth; pour on the isinglass $\frac{1}{2}$ pt. of boiling water; boil it down one-half, add it to the cream very hot, beat in thoroughly, then turn it into the moulds.

LEMON JELLY.

1 paper of Cox's gelatine, 3 pints of boiling water; stir until all is dissolved; then add $1\frac{1}{2}$ lbs of sugar, 5 lemons cut in small pieces, strain all through a flannel bag.

COCOANUT CREAM.
Mrs. J. W. Clark.

$\frac{1}{4}$ paper Cox's refined isinglass dissolved in 1 pt. of boiling water, 1 pt. of scalded milk and the yolks of 2 eggs, with 2 tablespoonfuls of sugar well beaten ; beat the whites of 2 eggs with 2 tablespoonfuls of sugar ; when cold, mix together with 1 qt. of cream, 1 teacup of sugar, 1 tablespoon of vanilla, and sprinkle over the top 1 teacup of cocoanut; keep cold until served.

PIE-PLANT JELLY.

Mrs. E. S. W.

Pick the plant while tender and juicy ; boil, being careful not to scorch ; add as many lemons sliced as you wish ; strain through a flannel bag, without squeezing ; add to every 3 pts. of juice 2 pts. of sugar, or a lb to a pint if preferred. Boil it until it jellies nicely.

QUINCE JELLY.

Mrs. Wm. Moore.

Take parings of quinces and apples, about ½ apple, put in a kettle and pour in water to almost cover, after being pressed down ; cook until tender, then strain through a flannel bag; to a measure of this juice, take an equal measure of white sugar, when the juice has been well strained add half the sugar and after it has commenced to boil let it boil hard 20 minutes—no longer—add the other half of sugar, and when it has reached the boiling point again let it boil briskly fifteen minutes, and 'tis done. Straining it a second time improves it, but is not necessary.

CRAB APPLE JELLY.

Cut Siberian crab apples in pieces, but do not pare them, cover them with water and stew until soft ; pour them into a jelly bag and strain ; to 3 pts. of juice add 2¼ pts. sugar ; boil until it jellies ; pour in glasses and set in the sun ; cover air tight.

SPICED PEACHES.

Mrs. M. Firmstone.

To 7 lbs of peaches, take 3 lbs of sugar, 1 pint of good vinegar, boil the sugar and vinegar, pour it over the peaches, and let them stand over night, then boil until clear, adding ½ an oz. each of unground cloves and cinnamon.

SPICED TOMATOES.

One peck of tomatoes ; 1 lb of brown sugar ; 1 pint of vinegar ; a dessertspoonful of mace ; a tablespoonful each of cloves and cinnamon. After having removed the skin, put the tomatoes on to boil, and as they begin to boil, pour off the juice, that they may not be watery, then add the other ingredients, and cook until perfectly done. Time one hour.

SPICED CURRANTS.
Mrs. Wm. Van Wagenen.

5 lbs of currants ; 3 lbs of sugar ; 1 pint of vinegar ; 1 tablespoonful of salt ; 1 tablespoonful of pepper ; 1 tablespoonful of cloves ; 1 tablespoonful of cinnamon ; 1 tablespoonful of allspice. Boil slowly half an hour.

CRANBERRY SAUCE.

½ gallon of cranberries, picked and washed ; 1 qt. of water ; stew slowly until soft ; strain the pulp through a cullender or sieve ; sweeten to taste, but be sure to have it sweet enough.— Eat with roast turkey, game and meats.

APPLE SAUCE.

Pare and slice some ripe tart apples ; stew in enough water to cover them, until they are soft ; mash and press through a cullander ; while hot, add a small lump of butter ; sweeten to taste. If you wish, grate in nutmeg.

AMBROSIA.

12 sweet oranges peeled and sliced ; 1 grated cocoanut—remove the dark part next the shell ; 1 cup of white powdered sugar ; place some of the oranges in a glass bowl, then some of the cocoanut ; sprinkle sugar over this ; repeat this until all is used, reserving some of the cocoanut and sugar for top.

SUGARED ORANGES.

Pare and cut the oranges into thin slices, removing the seeds, then cover thickly with powdered white sugar. Lemons may be prepared in the same way if desired.

TO STEW PEARS.

Pare them, cut in half, put them in a stew pan with very little water; let them stew until tender, add a small teacup of sugar to a quarter of a peck of pears; let them stew until the syrup is rich; a lemon boiled with the pears and sliced when the sugar is added, improves color and flavor.

STEWED PRUNES.

Wash, and put them into a porcelain-lined kettle, with sufficient boiling water to cover them; let them stand for two or three hours to swell, then place them on the range, or stove, in the same water in which they were steeped; let them simmer slowly, and when done, sweeten to taste.

APPLE BUTTER.
Mrs. M. J. G.

Wash and drain some apples, then cut them in pieces, and take out the cores and specks; stew until tender, and when cold rub through a coarse sieve; add to each pint of the pulp (that has passed through the sieve), ¾ of a pound of sugar, and cook until clear. Add spices to taste, a few minutes before it is done.

TOMATO BUTTER.
Miss E. Bell.

½ peck of nice tart apples; 1½ pecks of ripe tomatoes; 2 large lemons, cut fine; 1 oz. of white ginger cut fine; sweeten to taste, with sugar; boil down thick, and stir constantly.

TO STEW APPLES WHOLE.

Peel and core the apples; make a syrup of 1 pt. of water to 1 pt. sugar; when boiling, put in the apples, being careful not to break them; cook until tender.

ORANGE MARMALADE.
Mrs. Mary E. Draper.

Weigh the oranges and allow pound for pound of sugar; pare the rind of half the oranges as thinly as possible, putting it into a bucket with plenty of cold water; cover tightly, and boil slowly until soft enough to pierce easily with a straw; in the meantime, grate the rinds of the other half, and set aside; squeeze the juice of the oranges, being careful to exclude the seeds; put the sugar into a kettle with little less than half a pint of water to each pound of sugar; skim, while boiling, till clear and thick; take the boiled parings and cut into small shreds; put them in the clarified sugar and boil 10 minutes; then add the pulp, juice and grated rind and boil all together 20 minutes, or until it is a transparent mass.

CURRANT, STRAWBERRY, OR RASPBERRY JAM.

Let the fruit be very ripe, pick it clean from the stalks, bruise it, and to every pound of fruit put ¾ of a pound of sugar; stir it well, and boil half an hour.

APPLE BUTTER.

6 bus. good apples, pared and cut fine; 3 gals. of good syrup; 4 gals. of water; 1 lb cinnamon, ground fine, just before removing from the fire.

QUINCE BUTTER.

1 bushel of quinces, cut fine; ½ bushel of apples, 1 gal. of syrup, 1 gal. water.

RASPBERRY JAM.
Mrs. Wm. Van Wagenen.

To each lb. of raspberries, ¾ lb of sugar; scald together, after which pour into tin pans, not more than 2 inches thick; cover with gauze or some thin material, and place them in the hot sun a couple of days; they retain their color and flavor.

cooked in this way, and are much nicer than cooked over a fire

TOMATO HONEY.

Mrs. J. W. Collins.

For each ℔ of tomatoes allow the grated peel of 1 lemon, and 6 fresh peach leaves; boil until the leaves are to pieces; strain to each ℔ of liquid 1 ℔ of loaf sugar and juice of one. lemon; cook half an hour, or until a thick jelly; put in glasses, and lay double tissue paper over them.

PRESERVES.

GENERAL DIRECTIONS.

Have all your vessels clean and dry.

Iron, coated with earthenware, makes the nicest kettle.

It is best to have a small stand between the kettle and the stove, thus there will be no danger of burning, and the cook be spared much trouble.

Skim off all scum as it rises.

It is considered best, in jams and jellies, to boil and reduce them some before the sugar is added.

Do not use a tin or iron spoon to stir jelly.

It is not easy to give time of boiling jelly; this depends on the condition of the fruit, etc.

By taking out a spoonful in a saucer and setting it in cold water, the state of the jelly can be easily found out.

Tin pans alter the color of any fruit.

Choose a dry day to gather fruit for jelly.

PEACH PRESERVES.

Take fine large peaches, pare them carefully, and to 1 ℔ of fruit take ¾ of a ℔ of white sugar; leave the peaches whole, or divide if you like; make the syrup in a porcelain-lined, or perfectly bright brass kettle, and lay the fruit in; cook slowly until the peaches are clear, then lift out carefully into your jar; cook the syrup down and pour over.

TOMATO PRESERVES.

Take the small pear tomatoes, and scald them by pouring boiling water over them; let them stand until cool, then make a syrup of white sugar, and when boiling hot put them in one pound of sugar to one pound of tomatoes, and simmer until they become transparent, and flavor with lemon or ginger.

WATERMELON PRESERVES.

Soak the melon in salt and water one week—three days in clear water; then boil in alum water, covering them very thick with grape leaves, until perfectly green; then throw in clear cold water, and change the water every day; make a thin syrup of half a pound of sugar to the pound, and boil them in it until nearly done, then make a rich syrup, a pound of sugar to a pound of fruit, and boil until transparent; make strong ginger tea, strain it and wet the sugar with it. Season with mace.

TO PRESERVE PEARS.

Take small, rich fruit as soon as the pips are black; set them on the fire in a kettle with water to cover them; let them simmer until they yield to the pressure of the fingers; remove with a skimmer, and put them in cold water; pare them neatly, leave on a small bit of the stem and the blossom end, and pierce them to the core at the blossom end; make a syrup of one pound of sugar to one pound of fruit—less sugar, if preferred; when it is boiling hot pour it over the pears; let it stand until the next day; heat the syrup again to a boil, and pour over the pears; let them stand a day or two, put them on the fire and boil gently until the pears are clear; put them in jars, boil the syrup until thick, and pour it over them.

CITRON PRESERVES.
Mrs. A. McFarland.

To every pound of citron take ¾ ℔ of sugar; slice the citron and cover with weak alum water over night; then boil in clear water until tender, then make a syrup of the sugar and put it in and boil slowly until transparent; add ginger root or sliced lemon to your taste—must be put in while the preserves are cooking.

PRESERVES—ORANGES AND LEMONS.

Rub all the oil out of the oranges with hard lumps of sugar (scrape it off of the sugar with a knife into a glass jar, it is nice for flavoring,) then cut a slit on one side an inch long, take out all the seeds with the handle of a teaspoon; soak in weak salt water for eight days, changing the water daily; soak a day in clear water, and boil in clear water, until you can pierce them with a straw; weigh them, and to 1 lb of fruit allow 2 lbs of sugar; divide the sugar in four parts; make a syrup of one part; boil the fruit in it ten minutes; the next day let the fruit only scald, boiling the syrup longer, and pour hot over the fruit; repeat this every other day, adding the sugar each day, until the fruit is clear, and the syrup thick and rich. Pursue the same rule with the lemons.

PRESERVED CHERRIES.

To every pound of the seeded fruit, take $\frac{3}{4}$ of a lb of white sugar, cook twenty minutes from the time they commence boiling, then put hot into jars and seal. Strawberries are very nice preserved in the same way, only adding a little bit of alum to harden the fruit.

PRESERVED STRAWBERRIES.

2 lbs of strawberries; 2 lbs of sugar; alum, size of small nutmeg; boil the sugar and berries together for eight minutes, then add the alum, and let them boil seven minutes longer; take the strawberries out and let the juice boil for five minutes more. The alum hardens the fruit. Not more than 2 lbs of fruit should ever be boiled at a time.

 PICKLES.

YELLOW PICKLES.
Mrs. Dickinson.

1 gallon of vinegar or more, in a 4 gallon jar; ½ pint of white mustard seed; 2 oz. of turmeric; 1 oz. of mace; 4 oz. of white ginger; 2 tablespoonfuls of celery seed; 3 oz. of black pepper, whole; 2 tablespoonfuls of coriander seed; all these spices to be well beaten; one large double handful of horseradish; 1 tablespoonful of salt; 6 lbs of coarse brown sugar; 3 lemons sliced; lay the ginger in salt water over night; slice it and spread it to dry; take Early Yorks, if small, halve them, if large, cut in quarters; to be kept in brine, that will bear an egg, three days; scald in clear water until tender; squeeze dry, then throw in a jar of inferior vinegar, or half vinegar and water, colored with turmeric, for two days, then place layers of cabbage and layers of sugar in your preserving kettle, (porcelain lined,) cover with the spiced vinegar, until all the sugar is dissolved, then throw all in the spiced vinegar. Take 2 qts. of small white onions, boil and soak in salt and water until tender, then boil in weak milk and water, to extract the onion taste. Put in the jar of yellow pickles.

DAMSON PICKLES.
Mrs. Dickinson.

To 1 lb of the fruit, add 1 lb of sugar, 1½ pints of vinegar, with half an ounce of mace and cloves; boil the syrup every day for six mornings, and pour hot over the fruit.

PEACH PICKLES.
Mrs. D.

To 3 lbs of peaches allow 2 lbs of sugar, 1 pint of vinegar, 1 tablespoonful of cloves, 1 of cinnamon, 1 oz. of mace; boil the vinegar with the sugar and spice, and pour every day, (for five mornings) over the fruit.

PICKLES.

36 cucumbers, medium size; in salt six or seven days, then take out and rinse, and chop with two cabbage heads; let it remain over night; rinse and drain off, then chop four heads of celery with it; 1 pint of grated horseradish; 2 oz. of cinnamon, 6 tablespoons of ground mustard; 1 cup of sugar; bottle, putting good cider vinegar with it. Cork tight.

PICCALILLI.
Mrs. E. B. Moore.

¼ peck of tomatoes; 1 head of cabbage; 2 doz. cucumbers; 1 doz. green peppers; ½ doz. onions; slice the onions and let them stand ten minutes with boiling water over them; chop fine, and separate the rest of the ingredients; sprinkle salt to suit the taste; after adding all together, let the mixture stand one hour, after which, press it dry, then pour cold vinegar on it, let this stand 24 hours, then drain it all off, and to every gallon of the mixture, add ½ lb of sugar; use mustard seed, cloves, mace, and enough vinegar to cover it. To be poured on boiling hot.

PICKLED CURRANTS.
Mrs. H. A. T.

1 lb fruit, after draining; 1 lb of sugar; 2 tablespoonfuls of vinegar; 1 teaspoonful of cinnamon; ½ teaspoonful of cloves; boil all together two or three hours; pick the currants from the

stems, after draining all the juice you can without much pressing, then weigh the fruit.

MARTINO PICKLES.

Soak well in a brine for 1 week, boil gently till tender in weak vinegar, in an iron kettle; scald some allspice, horseradish and pepper; put layers of onions between the martinoes, and pour over them the hot vinegar. Fit for use in six weeks. It is very important to watch the bushes closely to gather the fruit before they become fibrous. Gather them early in the morning while the dew is on them.

PICKLED PLUMS.

1 quart of vinegar; 4 lbs of sugar; 7 lbs of plums; 1 oz. of cloves; 1 oz. of cinnamon; wipe each plum, and stick two or three cloves in each plum, put them in a jar, then put the sugar, vinegar and cinnamon over a fire and let come to a boil, then pour it over the plums the next day; scald the syrup again, and the third time put plums and all over the fire, and let them come to a boil.

GREEN TOMATO PICKLES.

Mrs. O. F. Moore.

1 peck of green tomatoes, sliced very thin; sprinkle with salt; rest 24 hours; drain, then take six onions, cut in the same way, and at the same time; mix together ¼ lb of mustard seed (white;) 1 oz. of ground pepper; 1 oz. of cloves; 1 oz. of ground ginger; 1 oz. of ground mustard; put a layer of tomatoes and one of spice alternately in a preserving kettle; add ½ lb of moist sugar; cover with vinegar; boil gently until transparent; when cold it is ready for use.

PICKLED ONIONS.

Put the onions into salt and water for nine days, observing to change the water every day, next put them into jars, and pour fresh boiling salt and water over them; cover them close up till they are cold, then drain the onions and put them into bottles; fill them up with cider vinegar; put into every bottle a slice or two of ginger, a blade of mace, and a teaspoonful of sweet oil, which will keep the onions white. Cork them tight. Keep in a dry place.

CUCUMBER PICKLES.

Cover the cucumbers with brine (made of water and salt, strong enough to bear up an egg) 24 hours, then wash in clear water and dry them; place some cucumbers in the jar; add ginger, horseradish, and pepper pods; add more cucumbers and spices, until the jar is full; boil cider vinegar and pour over. Cover tight.

SPANISH PICKLES.
Mrs. C. G. Young.

One half bushel full grown cucumbers; cut an inch thick; thick; put them in layers a finger length in depth; 1 oz. white pepper; 1 oz. of mace; 1 oz. of turmeric; 1 oz. of cloves; 1 oz. of cinnamon; 1 oz. of celery seed; 1 oz. of ginger; $\frac{1}{2}$ oz. of red pepper; 1 oz. of allspice; $\frac{1}{2}$ oz. of black mustard seed; $\frac{1}{2}$ lb of white mustard seed; 1 handful of salt with each layer of spices between the layer of cucumbers; there may be added yellow ochre; $\frac{1}{2}$ peck of onions, sliced; 2 boxes of mustard; 1 lb of brown sugar; pour strong, cold vinegar over them. They must be stirred frequently. While warm weather, after mixed, boil two hours.

TO PICKLE GREEN WALNUTS.
Mrs. M. J. Gaylord.

Gather the walnuts, or what is better, butternuts, when very small; prick them several times through and through, pack them in alternate layers of salt and nuts; when they have made a brine, drain them, and repack with fresh salt; let them remain eight days; wash free from salt, and wipe them; lay them to dry three days; steep spices in strong vinegar, heat it boiling hot and pour it over the nuts; let them stand one week, then pack the nuts in jars with spices; heat good vinegar near to boiling heat, fill the jars, let them become entirely cold, and then cork tightly; the vinegar can be used in fish sauces after the pickles are used.

PLUM PICKLES.
Mrs. E. B M.

6 lbs of sugar; 7 lbs of plums; 1 qt. of vinegar; 2 even spoonfuls of cloves; 1 even spoonful of cinnamon; scald the vinegar, sugar, cloves and cinnamon together, and pour on the plums. Let them stand ten days, then pour off and scald it again.

GREEN PICKLES.
Mrs. Dickinson.

2 gallons of vinegar, in a four gallon jar; ½ pint of black mustard seed; 4 ounces of ginger in sticks; 2 ounces of long peppers; 1 oz. of cinnamon; 2 oz. of stick cinnamon; 3 oz. of allspice; 1 oz of cloves; 1 large double handful of horseradish; 1 oz. of mace; 1 spoonful of salt; 6 lbs of brown sugar; 3 lemons sliced; 2 tablespoonfuls each of celery and coriander seed; all to be well beaten. Put the cucumbers in salt and water a week or more, then green with grape leaves and vinegar and water; cover close and keep hot until sufficiently colored, then throw them in a jar of weak vinegar, to extract the salt, then put them in the spiced vinegar.

STUFFING FOR FORTY MANGOES.
Mrs. Dickinson.

1lb of ginger; 1 oz. of mace; 1 lb of mustard seed; 1 oz. of nutmegs; 1 lb of horseradish; 2 oz. of turmeric; 1 lb chopped onions; 1 handful of black pepper; mix these ingredients into a paste with a quarter of a pound of ground mustard, and a cup of sweet oil, and 1 lb of brown sugar. Put a clove of garlic into each mango; take the mangoes, wash them and cut out a little plug, remove all the seeds, replace the plug, or square, tie with strips of cotton or twine, to keep them in place; put in salt and water for a day or two, then boil in clear water until they are tender enough to pierce with a straw. When cold, stuff each one; add the plug; sew it on with a coarse thread and needle, and wrap with a string, and cover with cold vinegar. So many persons object to the flavor of oil, it is well to omit it, and add the juice of lemon.

CHOW-CHOW.
Mrs. A. W. Buskirk.

¼ pk. of green tomatoes; 1 doz. onions; 1 doz. cucumbers; ½ doz. green peppers; 1 head cabbage; 10 cts. worth of horse-radish; mustard, salt, celery; cover with good vinegar and boil slowly two hours, stirring often.

CHOW-CHOW.
Mrs. W. A. Hutchins.

¼ peck of green tomatoes; half quantity white onions; 1 doz. cucumbers; same number of green peppers; 1 head cabbage; season with mustard, celery seed, and salt to taste; boil two hours in good cider vinegar; cover tight when done.

CHOW-CHOW.

3 large cabbage heads; ½ pt. white mustard seed; ½ pt. horse-

radish; 1 teacup of white sugar; ½ teacup salt; 1 pod of red pepper; put in jar, and cover with cold vinegar.

Pepper Sauce.

PEPPER VINEGAR.

Take 6 large red peppers, slit them up, and boil in 3 pints of strong vinegar; boil down to 1 qt., strain and bottle. Will keep for years.

PEPPER SAUCE.

1 doz. of peppers (green), 9 cucumbers, 3 heads of cabbage, 6 onions, if you want them, 1 doz. tomatoes, all chopped pretty fine; whole white and brown mustard seed, and whole cloves; cover with vinegar.

CATSUP.

TOMATO CATSUP.

Take ½ peck of tomatoes, wash and slice them, put them in your preserving kettle, and let them stew gently until quite soft, but do not stir them; strain the juice through a sieve, pour it back into the kettle; add 2 doz. cloves, ½ oz. of allspice, ½ oz of mace, salt and cayenne to your taste; boil it down half; next day strain out the spice, and to every pint of juice add ½ gill of good vinegar, and bottle for use.

TOMATO CATSUP.
Mrs. H. A. Towne.

Boil 1 bushel of tomatoes until tender; rub through a cullender, add 2 qts. of cider vinegar, 1¼ lbs of salt, ¼ lb of black pepper, ½ lb of allspice, 2 oz. of cayenne pepper, 6 onions, 3 grated nutmegs, 3 lbs of brown sugar; boil down, and when done strain through a sieve to remove onions; bottle.

TOMATO CATSUP.
S. E. F.

½ bushel of skinned tomatoes; 1 qt. of vinegar; 1 lb of salt; ¼ lb of black pepper, 2 oz. of cayenne; ¼ lb allspice; 1 oz. of cloves; 3 boxes of mustard; 20 cloves of garlic; 6 onions; 2 lbs of brown sugar, 1 handful of peach leaves; boil 3 hours, constantly stirring it, strain it through a fine sieve or coarse cloth, then bottle it.

TOMATO SAUCE.
Mrs. C. S. Smith.

18 large tomatoes, ripe; 2 green peppers; 2 large onions; 4 cups of vinegar; 2 tablespoonfuls of salt; 5 tablespoonfuls of sugar, 2 of ginger, 2 of cloves, 2 of cinnamon, 2 of allspice, 1 nutmeg; cook 1 hour.

CUCUMBER CATSUP.
Miss E. Bell.

Take 12 full-grown cucumbers, lay them one hour in cold water, pare and grate them into an earthen vessel; season with pepper, salt and vinegar, making it the consistency of marmalade; when mixed well transfer to glass jar, making air tight.

GOOSEBERRY CATSUP.

Boil the gooseberries in as little water as possible, then strain through a fine sieve; add 7 coffee cups of pulp, 5 cups of sugar, 2 teaspoonfuls of cinnamon and 3 of cloves; put in a wide-mouthed bottle.

CHILTON SAUCE.
Mrs. T. J. Graham.

½ peck of tomatoes; 4 peppers; 2 onions, chopped fine; grated horseradish to taste; 2 cups of vinegar; 2 tablespoons of salt, 2 of sugar, 2 of cloves, (ground), 2 of ginger (ground); 1 nutmeg, grated; cinnamon to suit the taste; boil one hour and bottle; if to be kept long, seal it.

WALNUT CATSUP.

Take green walnuts, before the shell is formed, pound them in a marble mortar, squeeze out the juice through a coarse cloth; put to every pound of juice 1 lb of anchovies, 1 lb of bay salt, 1 oz. of cayenne, 2 oz. of black pepper; of mace, cloves, and ginger, each 1 oz., and a stick of horse-radish; boil together until reduced to half the quantity; put it into a pot, and when cold, bottle it; it will be ready for use in three months.

Coffee, Chocolate and Tea.

TO MAKE GOOD TEA.
Mrs. C. S. Smith.

See that the water boils; scald the pot, put in a teaspoonful for each person; pour a little water upon green tea, and let it stand two or three minutes where it will keep hot; then fill the pot with boiling water; green tea should not be boiled, and it is rendered dead by steeping too long; use the same quantity of black tea, and fill the pot with boiling water; then set on the stove to boil up once. Green and black mixed are good.

TO BROWN COFFEE.

After picking it over carefully, put it into a bread pan and place in the oven of your stove; while it is browning do not attempt to do anything else, but watch it closely and stir every few moments, that the grains may all brown evenly; when done, it should be a chestnut brown.

HOW TO MAKE GOOD COFFEE.
Mrs. A. McFarland.

To each person take one tablespoonful of ground coffee (and one for the coffee pot) and one large teacup of boiling water to each person; first scald the coffee pot and then put in the coffee, add the white of an egg and a little cold water; stir well, and add the boiling water; let it boil from five to ten minutes, when put in a little cold water and lift it off to settle. Coffee, when boiled too long, tastes like cold coffee warmed over.

CHOCOLATE.

1 qt. of new milk, or milk and cream; ¾ of a cake of sweet German chocolate; break up the chocolate into small bits; let the milk get scalding hot, and then add the chockolate, stir constantly until the chocolate is dissolved to prevent its burning or sticking to the bottom of the vessel. After it is thoroughly dissolved let it boil about two minutes, remove it from the fire and in case 'tis too strong for the taste dilute with boiling milk or cream. The safest plan is to serve as it is, and allow each to add the cream for themselves.

CAKES.

GENERAL DIRECTIONS.

Have your oven ready as soon as your cake is mixed. It makes a cake less light to stand, particularly those having soda or baking powder in them.

Fruit must be well dried, and dusted with flour; if put in damp, will make it heavy.

Use good white sugar, if you want your cake nice. Some cooks sift the sugar. Coffee sugar makes good common cake. Eggs should be fresh, and beaten very light. Use none but good butter, the least strong flavor will be present in the cake.

Cake cannot be beaten too much. An earthen or wooden bowl is best. Tin is too cold, and the cake will not beat so light.

In winter, warm the flour.

Be careful in measuring and weighing. A very small mistake will sometimes ruin a cake.

Try your cake with a broomstraw. If it comes out free from dough, it is done; if it sticks, leave it in longer.

Too little flour or too cold an oven makes sad cake.

It will keep nicely to wrap it in a linen cloth and put it in a stone jar.

Some beat cake with the hand, others prefer a spoon.

CITRON CAKE.
Mrs. B. B. Gaylord.

1½ lbs of butter; 1½ lbs of sugar; 1½ lbs of flour; 13 eggs; 1 gill of rose-water; the grating of 1 nutmeg; 2 lbs of citron, cut thin and small; beat the butter and sugar until very light, then add the yolks of the eggs, with the rose-water and one-half of the flour; whisk the whites of the eggs as lightly as possible, and add alternately with the remaining flour, and lastly stir in the citron, previously floured. Bake in one large, or two small cakes; cover the pans with buttered paper. Bake in a moderate oven.

CITRON CAKE.

1 lb of sugar; ¾ lb of flour; 6 oz. of butter; whites of 14 eggs; ½ lb of citron, sliced thin, and floured; juice of 1 lemon, and grated rind; small cup of milk; bake 20 minutes. Place a layer of dough and one of citron, and so on.

FRUIT CAKE.
Mrs. M. J. Gaylord.

2 lbs of flour; 2 lbs of white sugar; 2 lbs of butter; 20 eggs; 3 lbs of currants, washed and dried; 3 lbs of raisins, seeded and cut; 1 lb of citron, cut fine; ½ lb. almonds, blanched and

chopped; 1 gill of rose-water; 2 nutmegs, and a little mixed spice; work the butter to a cream, mix the sugar and spice, and work all well together; then separate the eggs and beat the yolks lightly, and add with part of the flour to butter and sugar; then add the remainder of the flour and whites of the eggs, beaten to a stiff froth; next, add the rose-water; then the currants, raisins, citron and almonds (previously floured); mix all thoroughly but lightly together, and put into a pan lined with buttered paper. Bake four hours and a half.

FRUIT CAKE, WITHOUT BUTTER OR EGGS.
Mrs. H. A. Towne.

1 lb. of fat pork, either fresh or salt; 3 cups of brown sugar; 1 teaspoonful of soda; 2 teaspoonfuls each of cinnamon, cloves and allspice; 1 nutmeg; fruit to taste (or 1 lb. raisins, ½ lb. citron); chop the pork very fine; add one cup of boiling water, one cup of sugar; stir well, together; then add another cup of boiling water, and the rest of the sugar; make stiff as cup-cake with flour—about 5½ cups.

BLACK CAKE.
Mrs. W. Van Der Lyn.

1 lb. of sugar; 1 lb. of butter; 10 eggs; beat them well together; 2 nutmegs; 2 tablespoonfuls of cloves; 3 tablespoonfuls of cinnamon; 1 tablespoonful of mace; 2 lbs. of raisins; 2 lbs. of currants; ¼ lb. of citron; ½ teaspoonful soda to ½ cup sweet milk.

WHITE FRUIT CAKE.
Mrs. Manly.

Whites of 16 eggs; 1 lb. of sugar; ¾ lb. of butter; 1 lb. of flour; 1 teaspoonful of extract of bitter almonds; 1 lb. of blanched almonds (sweet); 2 oz. bitter almonds; pound the almonds in a mortar, with a little rose-water to prevent oiling; 1 lb. citron, cut fine; 1 cocoanut, grated; whisk the eggs until they will stand alone; cream the butter, into which stir flour, until quite stiff; then add alternately egg, sugar and flour, till all are well combined; flavor with vanilla, or extract of bitter almonds; flour the fruit, and stir in last. Bake in a slow oven, using great caution not to burn it. Ice.

FRUIT CAKE.
Mrs. A. McFarland.

2½ lbs of butter; 2½ lbs. of sugar; 2½ pounds of flour; 5 lbs. of raisins; 5 lbs. of currants; 1 lb. of citron; 2 lbs. of almonds, blanched, and cut in small pieces; 3 nutmegs; 2 oz. of cinnamon; 20 eggs; mix all the ingredients thoroughly, and bake from four to five hours in a slow oven.

MEASURE BLACK CAKE.
Mrs. H. L. Miller.

1 cup of butter; 3 cups of sugar; 3 eggs; ½ pt. of milk; 3 cups of flour; 1 lb. raisins; ½ lb. of currants; ½ lb. citron; nutmeg; cloves and cinnamon; 2 teaspoonfuls baking powder.

FRUIT CAKE.
Mrs. Manly.

1 lb. of sugar; 1 lb. of butter; 1 lb. of flour; 1 lb. of raisins; 1 lb. of currants; 1 lb. of citron; 8 eggs; beat the butter and sugar to a cream; add 2 eggs and a little flour, till all are used. Then add the fruit, which must always be floured. Use the above, minus the fruit, for pound cake.

FRUIT CAKE.

4 cups of butter; 8 cups of sugar; 12 cups of flour; 20 eggs; 2 nutmegs; 2 lbs. of raisins; 2 lbs. of citron; 2 lbs. of currants; 1 teaspoonful of cloves; 4 teaspoonfuls of cinnamon; 1 teaspoonful of mace; dredge the fruit in part of the flour; stir in the fruit last before baking. Bake four hours.

FRUIT CAKE.
Mrs. A. Pursell.

1 lb. of brown sugar; ¾ lbs. of butter; 1 lb. of flour; 2

lbs. of raisins; 2 lbs. of currants; ½ lb. of citron; 1 oz. of cloves; ½ oz. of mace; ½ pt. of sour cream; 1 scant tablespoonful of soda; 1 teacup of dark jelly; dredge the fruit with flour, and bake 3 hours.

BLACK FRUIT CAKE.
Mrs. R. W. Manly.

1 lb. of flour; 1 lb. of butter; 1 lb. of sugar; 2 lbs. of raisins; 2 lbs. of currants; ¾ lb. of citron; 8 eggs; ¼ oz. of mace; ¼ oz. of cloves; ¼ oz. of nutmeg; ½ oz. of cinnamon; 1 tablespoonful of ginger; 1 cup of dark jelly; beat the butter and sugar to a cream, eggs to a froth; fruit and flour last; bake 2 hours in a moderate oven.

FRUIT CAKE.
Mrs. George Johnson.

1¼ lbs. of butter; 1¼ lbs. of sugar, 1¼ lbs. of flour; 12 eggs; 2 lbs. of raisins; 2 lbs. of currants; ½ lbs. of citron; spices.;

POUND CAKE.
Mrs. A. McF.

1 ℔ of sugar: 1 ℔ flour; ¾ ℔ butter; 9 eggs; 2 teaspoonfuls of baking powder. Flavor with lemon.

DELICATE CAKE.
Miss Nettie Shepard.

2 ℔s of white sugar; 2 ℔s of butter; 2 ℔s of flour, and the whites of 30 eggs; stir the sugar and butter until very light; beat the eggs until they will stand alone; add the flour and eggs alternately; flavor with lemon and bake in a moderate oven.

DELICATE CAKE.

4 cups of sugar; 2 cups of butter; 7 cups of flour; 1 cup of

sour milk; 1½ teaspoonfuls of soda in the milk; 3 teaspoonfuls of cream of tartar, well worked in flour; flavor to taste; 16 eggs, using the whites only.

DELICATE CAKE.

Mrs. J. R. Clarke, of Oxford, N. Y.

2 cups of sugar; 1 cup of butter; 1 cup of milk; 3 cups of flour; 1 cup of corn starch; whites of 8 eggs; 2 teaspoonfuls of cream of tartar; one teaspoonful of soda; flavoring as you like.

FRENCH LOAF CAKE.

1 lb of flour; 1 lb of raisins; 1 lb of currants; ½ lb of butter; ¾ lb of brown sugar; 1 teaspoon of soda; ½ teacup of molasses, same of milk; ½ dozen eggs; teaspoonful each of cloves, and cinnamon, and nutmeg. Bake from three to four hours in slow oven.

FRENCH LOAF CAKE.

1 lb raisins; 1 lb flour; 1 lb of currants; ½ lb of butter; ¾ lb of brown sugar; 1 teaspoon of soda; 1 cup of sour milk; 1 cup of molasses; 4 eggs; 1 teaspoon of alum, cloves, mace, nutmeg and other spices to suit the taste. Put the fruit in last, having it well rolled in flour.

COCOANUT CAKE.

Beat 12 eggs to a stiff froth, the whites and yolks sparately, then mix them together, and add to them, gradually, 1 lb of white sugar; beat this ten minutes, then stir in, very lightly, 1 lb of flour; must not be beaten after the flour is added; bake in jelly-cake pans, in a quick oven. THE MIXTURE.—Soak ½ box of Cox's gelatine one hour, then dissolve this in ½ teacup of water, by heating and pouring it over the gelatine, and stirring until the gelatine is dissolved. Beat one pint of very rich cream to a stiff froth, also the whites of 8 eggs; grate 2 cocoanuts; after the gelatine is cool, but not stiff, stir it into the beaten cream, and then add the grated cocoanut with enough white sugar to sweeten, and 1 teaspoonful of vanilla, then add the whites of the eggs. Spread this mixture between the cakes, and also on the top cake. Preserve a little of the grated cocoanut to sprinkle over the top.

COCOANUT CAKES.

Mrs. W. Van Der Lyn, of Oxford, N. Y.

1 coffeecup of sugar; $\frac{2}{3}$ teacup of butter; $\frac{1}{2}$ teacup of sweet milk; 4 eggs, leave out the whites of two; 2 small teacups of flour; 2 teaspoonfuls of cream of tartar; $\frac{1}{2}$ teaspoonful of soda. Bake in layers. FILLING.—Beat the two whites and make frosting, not quite as thick as for cake, spread between each layer, and sprinkle with either fresh or prepared cocoanut. If prepared cocoanut, soak in a very little milk two or three hours before using.

PLAIN COCOANUT CAKE.

Beat $\frac{3}{4}$ lb of sugar and $\frac{1}{2}$ lb of butter, to a cream, add gradually, $\frac{3}{4}$ lb of flour, the whites of twelve eggs, beaten to a stiff froth, and $\frac{1}{2}$ of a grated cocoanut; mix well with part of flour, one teaspoonful of cream of tartar, and $\frac{1}{2}$ teaspoonful of soda. ICING.—Whites of four eggs, sixteen tablespoonfuls of powdered sugar, and the rest of cocoanut grated.

COCOANUT CAKE.

$\frac{1}{2}$ lb. of flour; $\frac{1}{4}$ lb. of butter; $\frac{1}{2}$ lb. of sugar; 1 cup of milk; whites of 8 eggs, $\frac{1}{2}$ teaspoonful of soda; 1 teaspoonful of cream of tartar; mix the above thoroughly, and add 1 grated cocoanut. After the cake is frosted, sift a cup of grated cocoanut over the top.

COCOANUT CAKE.

Mrs. C. S. Smith.

6 eggs; 1$\frac{1}{2}$ cups of sugar; 2 cups of flour; 2 teaspoons of baking powder; lemon; $\frac{1}{2}$ of the cocoanut mixed with the cake;

whites of 3 eggs; the rest of the cocoanut; sugar enough to make sweet.

COCOANUT CAKE.

1 cup of butter; 2 cups of sugar; 1 cup of sweet milk; the whites of 7 eggs; 2 cups of flour; 1 teaspoonful of soda; 3 teaspoonfuls of cream of tartar; 1 cocoanut grated; the whites of 4 eggs; 2 cups of pulverized sugar (loaf,) for icing between the layers.

BOILED SPONGE CAKE.

Miss E. Bell.

1 lb of sugar; ¾ lb of flour; 7 eggs; 1 teacup of water; pour the water on the sugar and let it boil; beat the eggs separately and then beat together; when well mixed, pour over them the boiling sugar, and stir constantly until cold enough to add the flour. Bake in a loaf, in a moderate oven.

WHITE SPONGE CAKE.

Mrs. Mary E. Draper.

. Whites of 8 eggs; 1 large cup of granulated sugar; 1 large cup of flour; beat eggs very stiff on a large platter; stir into it the granulated sugar, adding the flour into which has been stirred one teaspoon of cream of tartar. Bake in a square pan, in a quick oven.

BERWICK SPONGE CAKE.

Ms. Wm. Balcom, Oxford, N. Y.

6 eggs; 3 cups of powdered white sugar; 4 even cups of sifted flour; 2 teaspoons of cream of tartar; 1 cup of cold water; 1 teaspoon of soda; 1 lemon; beat the eggs two minutes, and put in the sugar and beat five minutes more, then stir in the cream of tartar and two cups of the flour, and beat one minute; now dissolve the soda in the water and stir in, having grated the rind of the lemon; squeeze in half of the juice only; and finally, add the other two cups of flour and beat all one minute, and

put into deep pans in a moderate oven. There is considerable beating about this cake, but if itself does not beat all the sponge cakes you ever beat, we will acknowledge it to be the beating cake all around.

SPONGE CAKE.
Mrs. Wm. Van Wagenen, Oxford, N. Y.

4 eggs, the yolks and whites beaten separately; 1 cup of sugar; 1 cup of flour; 1 teaspoonful of cream of tartar; ½ teaspoon of soda. Flavor with vanilla.

ICE WATER SPONGE CAKE.

7 eggs; 3 cups of sugar; 3 cups of flour; 1 cup of ice water; beat the yolks and sugar together; add in water, then flour, lastly whites of eggs. Put eggs in ice water twenty minutes before using.

WHITE SPONGE CAKE.
Miss Hattie Damarin.

Whites of ten eggs; 1½ teacups of sugar; 1 cup of flour; 1 teaspoon of cream of tartar.

SPONGE CAKE.
Mrs. Ann L. Martin.

1 pint of sugar; 1 pint of flour; 3 large tablespoonfuls of water; 10 eggs. Sift in the flour last.

OLD VIRGINIA SPONGE CAKE.
Mrs. S. J. Glover.

10 eggs; 1 lb of pulverized sugar; 1 lemon; ⅝ lb. of sifted flour; beat the yolks of eggs very light; add sugar; beat half an hour; add juice of lemon, beat in well; beat the whites of eggs very stiff; stir in half of them gently; add half of flour, then the remainder of eggs; last, the remainder of flour; never beat while adding whites of eggs or flour, but stir in well as gently as possible; bake in a moderate oven three-fourths of an

hour. Place a bowl of water in the oven while baking the cake.

WHITE MOUNTAIN CAKE.
Miss E. Bell.

Whites of ten eggs or five whole eggs, two cups flour, one ounce white sugar, one and one-half cups butter, one teaspoon soda, two teaspoons cream tartar, one ounce of ammonia; bake in thin layers; use icing between. FOR ICING—one pint of white sugar boiled in a teacup of water; pour it over the whites of two eggs, beaten light.

WHITE MOUNTAIN CAKE.
Miss Clara Waller.

One cup of butter, two cups of sugar, three cups of flour, one-half cup sweet milk, whites of ten eggs, two teaspoonfuls of cream tartar, one of soda. Bake in three deep jelly cake pans. Spread icing between and all over the cake. ICING—Whites of four eggs and sixteen tablespoonfuls of powdered sugar. Flavor to taste.

ORANGE CAKE.
Mrs. H. L. Miller.

2 cups sugar, 2 cups flour, $\frac{1}{2}$ cup cold water, the yolks of five eggs, and the whites of 3 eggs, the juice and grated rind of one orange, 2 teaspoonfuls baking powders. Beat the yolks very light, then add the sugar and water; after beating thoroughly, then add the other ingredients and bake in jelly tins, in four layers. When cold, beat the whites of 2 eggs, stiffen with sugar, flavor with juice and rind of 1 orange, and spread thickly between layers.

STARCH CAKE.

7 eggs, whites only, 1 cup of butter, 1 cup of sweet milk, 2 cups of sugar, 1 cup of corn starch, 2 cups of flour, 1 teaspoon cream tartar, $\frac{1}{2}$ teaspoon soda. For flavor, use lemon or rose.

STARCH CAKE.
Mrs. C. S. Green.

3 cups of white sugar, 1 cup of starch, dissolved in 1 cup of

sweet milk, 1 cup of butter, whites of 12 eggs, salt, 3 teaspoons of baking powder, mixed in 3 cups of flour. Flavor to taste.

PLAIN MOUNTAIN CAKE.

Two eggs, beat separate, one-half cup of butter, two cups of sugar, one cup of milk, two and a half cups of flour, three even teaspoons of baking powder; bake in layers. Take whites of two eggs, beat light, thicken with sugar. Spread between the layers while hot.

CORN STARCH CAKE.

Mrs. J. W. Clarke, of Oxford, N. Y.

½ lb of sugar, ¼ lb of butter, whites of 8 eggs, ½ lb of corn starch, ½ teaspoonful of soda, 1 teaspoonful of cream tartar. Flavor with lemon or bitter almonds.

CUP CAKE.

1 cup of butter, 2 cups of sugar, 3 cups of flour, 4 eggs. Lemon extract.

CUP CAKE.

1 cup of butter, 2 cups of sugar, (rubbed to a cream,) 5 eggs, 1 cup of milk, 4 cups of flour, 1 teaspoonful of soda, 2 teaspoonfuls of cream tartar. Flavor with lemon.

CUP CAKE.

Mrs. J. W. Clarke.

3 cups of sugar, 1 cup of butter, 5 eggs, 1 cup of new milk, 2 cups of wheat flour, 1 cup of corn starch, 1 teaspoonful of soda, 2 teaspoonsfuls of cream of tartar, ½ teaspoonful of mace.

LEMON JELLY CAKE.

Mrs. Warner.

3 cups of sugar, 1 cup of milk, 5 eggs, 2½ cups of flour, 3 teaspoonfuls of baking powder. JELLY—1 lemon, 2 eggs, 5 or

6 small apples, 1 cup sugar. Let the jelly cook slow until it thickens.

LEMON JELLY CAKE.

2 cups of sugar, 3 cups of flour, ⅔ cups of butter, ½ cup of sweet milk, 1 teaspoonful of baking powder. JELLY FOR CAKE:—1 lemon, 1 cup sugar, 2 large apples, 1 egg.

LEMON JELLY CAKE.

Mrs. Leet.

2 cups of sugar, 1 cup of milk, 2½ cups of flour, 5 eggs, 3 teaspoons of baking powder. FOR JELLY—1 lemon, 2 eggs, 3 large apples, or 6 small ones, 1 cup sugar.

LEMON CAKE.

Mrs. Mary E. Draper.

3 cups of pulverized sugar, 4 cups of flour, 1 cup of butter, 1 cup of sweet milk, 5 eggs, 1 small teaspoonful of soda, 1 lemon. Beat butter and sugar well together, add the milk, juice and grated rind of lemon; stir in the white of eggs, well beaten, afterward the soda, put in dry, and lastly the flour.

LEMON JELLY CAKE.

Miss Emma T. Johnson.

2 cups of sugar, 1 of milk, 3 eggs, 3 cups of flour, 1 teaspoon of cream tartar, ½ teaspoon of soda. JELLY FOR SAME—1 cup of sugar, 1 egg, 1 apple, 1 lemon, grated; let it boil, and spread on the cake hot.

LEMON JELLY FOR CAKE.

Mrs. H. L. Miller.

2 eggs, 1 cup of sugar, 1 large lemon, juice, and rind grated, 3 tablespoonfuls of water. Beat these thoroughly together, and put in a tin basin and set within the uncovered top of the tea kettle, which must be kept boiling until the steam thickens it

sufficiently. Stir constantly. When cold, spread it between the layers of cake like any other jelly. This will make one loaf with four layers.

SILVER CAKE.
Mrs. Currie.

2 cups of sugar, ½ cup of butter, ¾ cup of milk, 2½ cups of flour, whites of 8 eggs, ¾ teaspoonful of soda, 1 teaspoonful of cream tartar.

WHITE CAKE.
Mrs Burwell.

Whites of 7 eggs, 2 cups of sugar, 1 cup of butter, 1 cup of sweet milk, 4½ cups of flour, 1 teaspoon of soda in a tablespoon of milk, 2 teaspoonfuls of cream tartar in the flour.

WHITE CAKE.
Mrs. Gates.

1½ large teacups even full of butter, 3 teacups of sugar, 6 large eggs, whites only, 1½ cups sweet milk, 5 cups sifted flour, (put in cups lightly,) 1 teaspoon of soda, 3 teaspoons of cream tartar; put the soda in milk, cream tartar in flour; stir your butter to a cream before putting in sugar, then stir butter and sugar well before adding milk, flour and eggs.

YELLOW CAKE.

4 cups of sugar, 1½ cups of butter, (scant,) 1 cup of sweet milk, the yolks of 16 eggs, 5 cups of flour, 2 teaspoonfuls of cream tartar, 1 teaspoonful of soda.

GOLD CAKE.

1 cup of butter, 2 cups of powdered sugar, yolks of 8 eggs, 1 cup of milk, (sour,) 1 teaspoonful of soda, in milk, 4 cups of flour, 2 teaspoonfuls of cream tartar. Flavor to suit the taste.

SPICE CAKE.

2 cups of sugar, 2 cups of flour, 1 cup of water, ½ cup of but-

ter, 2 eggs, ½ lb each raisins and currants, 1 spoonful of baking powder, 1 small pinch of soda.

SPICE CAKE.
Mrs. Dr. Cotton.

1 cup of butter, 3 cups of sugar, 4 cups of flour, 5 eggs, 1 cup of milk, 2 teaspoons of baking powder, 1 teaspoon of cinnamon, 1 teaspoon of cloves, 1 teaspoon of nutmeg.

SPICE CAKE.
Mrs. C. G. Young.

3 cups of sugar, 1½ cups of butter, 5 cups of flour, ¾ pint of milk, 6 eggs, ½ pint of molasses, 2 teaspoonfuls of baking powder 1 tablespoonful of cloves, cinnamon, allspice, nutmeg.

ALMOND CAKE.

1 lb of sugar ¾ lb of butter, 1 lb of flour, 10 eggs, 1 tablespoon of baking powder. CREAM FOR THIS CAKE—Yolks of 4 eggs, well beaten, 1 cup of sugar, 1 cup of sour cream, 1 teaspoon of baking powder, 2 lbs blanched almonds; add whites of eggs, well beaten. This quantity makes two cakes, six layers each.

ALMOND CAKE.

2 cups of sugar, 1 cup of butter, 1 cup of sweet milk, 4 cups of flour, 5 eggs, 2 teaspoons of cream tartar, 1 teaspoonful of soda. Bake in jelly cake pans, and when done, put in each a custard, made of 1 cup of sour cream, 1 egg, ½ lb almonds, (when shells taken off,) 1 tablespoon of sugar. Flavor with vanilla, all beaten together.

CHOCOLATE CAKE.
Mrs. W. Van Der Lyn.

2 cups of sugar; 1 cup of butter; yolks of 5 eggs and whites of 2; 1 cup of milk; 3½ cups of flour; ½ teaspoonful of soda; 1 teaspoonful of cream of tartar. Filling for the cake—The

whites of 3 eggs; 1½ cups of sugar; 3 tablespoonfuls of grated chocolate; 1 teaspoonful of vanilla.

CHOCOLATE CAKE.
Miss R. Nye.

1 lb. of sugar; 1 lb. of flour; ½ lb. of butter; 6 eggs, or whites of 8 eggs; 1 tablespoonful of baking powder in the flour; 1 cup of sweet milk. Dressing for cake—1¼ lb. of brown sugar; ¼ lb. of Baker's chocolate; 1 cup of cream; butter the size of an egg; vanilla.

CHOCOLATE CAKE.

1 cup of butter; 2 cups of sugar; 1 cup of milk; 1 cup of corn starch; 2 cups of flour; the whites of 7 eggs; 1 teaspoonful of cream tartar; ½ teaspoonful of soda; flavor to suit taste; to this, add ½ cup of chocolate.

CREAM CAKE.
Alice Terry.

¾ cups of butter; 2 cups of sugar; 3¼ cups of flour; ½ cup of sweet milk; 4 eggs; 2 teaspoonfuls of baking powder; bake in layers. When cold, spread between the following mixture— 1 pt. sweet milk; 2 tablespoonfuls corn starch; 1 egg; ¾ cup of sugar. Heat the milk to boiling, wet the corn starch with cold milk, stir it in the hot milk; beat the eggs and sugar, and stir them in; put it on the fire, and stir till it is very thick; when cold, flavor and spread between.

CREAM CAKE.

3 eggs; 1 teacup of sugar; 1 teacup of flour; 1 small teaspoonful of soda; 2 small teaspoonfuls of cream tartar; dissolve the soda in three tablespoonfuls of water, the cream tartar in the flour; stir in all the ingredients; and for the jelly take 1 pint of milk—leave out enough of the milk to dissolve 2 tablespoonfuls of corn starch; mix with the starch 2 eggs; put the pint of milk on the fire, let it come to the scald; then stir in

the eggs and starch until it thickens; then add ¾ of a teacup of sugar; let it cool, and when cold flavor with vanilla. Bake this cake in two pie-pans, and when done split them in two and spread on the jelly.

CUSTARD CAKE.

Miss Emma Bell.

Use any cake, such as cup, mountain or jelly; bake in layers. Put between the following custard—¾ pint of thick sour cream or milk; 1 lb. blanched almonds pounded fine; 1 vanilla bean, powdered fine; 4 eggs—beat them separately; mix 2 tablespoonfuls of sugar with the whites, and 2 with the yolks; mix all together cold, and put between layers of cake.

GINGER BREAD.

Mrs. Gibbs.

1 pint of molasses; 1 qt. of flour; ½ pint of warm water; 1 teaspoonful of soda; 1 tablespoonful of ginger; 1 teacup of butter; 1 egg and a little salt.

CORN BREAD.

Mrs. Gibbs.

1 qt. of buttermilk; 1 pint of meal; 3 eggs; 1 teaspoonful of soda; 1 tablespoonful of sugar; 1 teaspoonful of salt. Bake in a hot oven.

SOFT GINGERBREAD.

Mrs. T. S. Currie.

1 cup of butter; 1 cup of sugar; 1 pint of molasses; 5 eggs; 5 cups of flour; 1 cup of sour milk; 1 teaspoonful of soda, one-half in the molasses and one-half in the milk; 1 tablespoonful of strong ginger. Other spices to taste.

SOFT GINGER CAKE.

Mrs. George Johnson.

1 cup of butter; 1 cup of sugar; 1 cup of molasses; 1 cup of sour milk; 3 eggs; 1 teaspoonful of soda in milk, and one in

molasses; 2 teaspoonfuls of cream of tartar in flour; flour enough to make the consistency of cup cake; ginger.

MARK GINGER CAKES.
Mrs. H. A. Towne.

1 cup of butter; 2 cups of sugar; 1 egg; 1 teaspoonful of ginger; ¼ cup of sour milk; dessertspoonful of soda; as much flour as you can stir in with a spoon; roll out, mark, and bake quickly on baking tins.

SOFT GINGER CAKE.
Mrs. A. McFarland.

1 pint of New Orleans molasses; 1 teacup of sour milk; 1 tablespoonful of butter or lard; 1 tablespoonful of ginger; 3 cups of flour; 1 tablespoon of soda, one-half of which must be stirred into the molasses, and the other into the sour milk, until they foam, when the other ingredients are added and thoroughly stirred. Bake in a moderate oven.

DOUGHNUTS.

Take 1 teacup of raised sponge, (bread sponge;) ½ cup of lard or butter; 2 cups of sugar; 3 eggs; teaspoonful of salt; cinnamon and nutmeg to taste, and flour enough to work stiff; let it rise, and roll out thin, and cut as you fancy, and fry in hot lard.

CRULLERS.
Mrs. Wm. Van Wagenen.

2 cups of sugar; 2 eggs; 3 tablespoonfuls of shortening; 1 cup of sweet milk; nutmeg; flour enough to stiffen it. Fry in hot lard.

CRULLERS—PLAIN.
Mrs. J. R. Clarke.

1 qt. of flour; 1½ cups of sugar; 1 egg; 2 tablespoonfuls of melted lard or butter, or 3 tablespoonfuls of sour cream, which is better; ½ teaspoonful of soda, dissolved in a little warm water;

mix with sweet milk, making the paste as soft as you can well roll it out.

JUMBLES.

1 cup of butter; 2 cups of sugar; 3 eggs; ½ cup sour milk; ⅓ teaspoonful soda; spices. Mix dough soft, and bake quick.

DOUGHNUTS.

2 cups of sugar; 1 cup of sour milk; 1 teaspoon of soda; 3 eggs; lump of butter size of an egg; flour enough to make a stiff dough. Fry in hot lard.

QUAKER CAKE.

1 lb. of sugar; ½ lb. of butter; 1 lb. of flour; 5 eggs; 1 cup of sour milk.

COOKIES.

Mrs L. B. Dana.

1 cup of butter; 2 cups of sugar; 1 cup of sour milk or butter milk; 2 eggs; lemon; 1 teaspoonful of soda. Roll out thick, with as little flour as possible. Bake quickly. Dust coarse with sugar over before putting in oven.

COOKIES.

4 eggs; 3 cups of sugar; 1 cup of butter; ⅓ cup of milk; 1 teaspoonful of soda; nutmeg to suit taste, and knead soft as possible.

MOLASSES COOKIES.

Mrs. Wm. Balcom, of Oxford, N. Y.

2 cups of molasses; 1 cup of shortening; 2 tablespoonfuls of soda; 1 teaspoonful of ginger; 1 teaspoonful of alum; 1 teaspoonful of cream tartar; 1 cup of hot water; half of water on soda, and half on the alum.

Miscellaneous Cakes.

MARBLE CAKE.

BLACK CAKE.—Yolks of 7 eggs; 2 cups of brown sugar; 2 cups of molasses; 1 cup of butter; 1 cup of sour milk; 5 cups of flour; 1 teaspoon of soda; 2 teaspoons of cinnamon; cloves, allspice and nutmeg.

WHITE CAKE.—Whites of 7 eggs; 2 cups of sugar; 1 cup of butter; 1 cup of sweet milk; 3 cups of flour; 1 teaspoon of soda; 2 teaspoons of cream of tartar. Flavor with lemon.

VANILLA CAKE.

3 eggs; ½ cup of butter; ½ cup of milk; 2 cups of flour; 1½ cups of sugar; 2 teaspoonfuls of baking powder; 1 teaspoonful of vanilla.

ALMOND MACAROONS.
Mrs. H. A. Towne.

Blanch ½ lb. of almonds, pound a few at a time in a mortar to a fine paste, with a little extract of lemon, or add to the paste an equal weight of white sugar, pulverized; whites of two eggs, not beaten; work it together with the back of a spoon till it is a nice paste, then dip your hand in water and roll into balls the size of a nutmeg; lay them an inch apart on white paper on a baking tin, passing a wet finger over each one, to smooth it; bake ¾ of an hour in a slow oven. Use grated cocoanut instead of almonds, if you wish.

MARBLE CAKE.
Mrs. Gibbs.

WHITE PART.—Whites of 4 eggs; 1 cup of white sugar; ½ cup of butter; ½ cup of sweet milk; 1 teaspoonful of cream of tartar; 2½ cups of flour. DARK PART.—Yolks of four eggs; 1 cup of brown sugar; ½ cup of molasses; ½ cup of butter; ½ cup of sour milk; 1 teaspoonful of soda; 2½ cups of flour, a little salt and plenty of spice.

BREAD CAKE.
Mrs. J. W. Clarke.

3 cups of bread dough; ⅔ cup of butter; 3 eggs; 2 cups of sugar; ¼ teaspoonful of soda, dissolved in butter; 1 lb. raisins; 1 teaspoonful of nutmeg; add a little flour; when well mixed, let it stand and rise an hour before baking.

SPLIT CAKE.
Mrs. Thomas.

1 pint of sour milk; a little salt; 1 tablespoon of lard; 1 tablespoon of butter, melted; 1 teaspoon of soda; just enough flour to roll; bake thick enough to split and butter. 'Tis splendid for strawberry cake.

NUT CAKE.
Mrs. J. W. Clarke.

2 cups of sugar; 1 cup of butter; 2 eggs; 1 cup of sour milk; 4 cups of flour; 1 teaspoonful of soda; ½ teaspoonful of cream of tartar; 1 pint of nut meats.

VELVET CAKE.
Miss Jennie McFarland.

1 lb. of sugar; 1 lb. of flour; ½ lb. of butter; 5 eggs; dis-

solve a light teaspoon of soda in a cup of sweet milk; stir a teaspoon of cream of tartar in the flour; flavor with lemon or vanilla, and bake one hour.

THANKSGIVING CAKE.

4 lbs. of light dough; 2 lbs. of sugar; 1 lb. of butter; 4 eggs; beat butter and sugar together one hour, divide it into two equal parts; work one-half in the dough; let it rise, then work in the other half, with the eggs well beaten; let it rise again, then add a spoonful of water, a teaspoon of soda, one nutmeg, one pound of raisins, 1½ lbs. of currants. Bake one hour and a half.

JUMBLES.
S. E. F.

3 cups of sugar; 1½ cups of butter; 1 cup of sweet milk; 5 cups of flour; 2 eggs; 1 small teaspoon of soda.

GINGER SNAPS.
Mrs. Harry Balcom.

1 cup of molasses; 1 cup of sugar; 1 cup of shortening; 1 tablespoon of ginger; 1 of soda, and 1 of vinegar; 1 egg and flour enough to roll good.

WEBSTER CAKE.

1 cup of sugar; 1 cup of molasses; 1 cup of milk; 1 egg; 1 teaspoon of soda; ¾ lb of raisins. Flour as in fruit cake.

GINGER SNAPS.
Mrs. Hull, of Oxford, N. Y.

1 cup of molasses; 1 cup of sugar; 1 tablespoonful of soda; 1 tablespoonful of ginger, then add a cup of melted butter, 1 egg; beat this well, then 3 cups of flour, then 1 tablespoonful of vinegar; beat thoroughly. Flour sufficient to roll out very thin.

COCOANUT DROPS.

½ lb. of grated cocoanut; ½ lb. of loaf sugar; whites of three eggs. Bake on white buttered paper, dropping the cakes at a little distance from each other.

HICKORY NUT CAKE.

½ cup of butter; 2 cups of sugar; 3 cups of flour; 1 cup of sweet milk; 2 cups of hickory nuts, cut fine; 1 teaspoon of vanilla; 2 teaspoons of baking powder; 4 eggs beaten separately.

HICKORY NUT CAKE.
Mrs. Jas. W. Newman.

1½ cups of sugar; ½ cup of butter; ⅔ cup of sweet milk; 2 cups of flour; 4 eggs (whites); 1 teaspoonful of cream tartar; ½ teaspoonful of soda; 2 cups of nuts.

BLACKBERRY CAKE.
Mrs. O. F. Moore.

1 cup of sugar; ¾ of a cup of butter; 3 eggs; 1½ cups of flour; 3 tablespoonfuls sour cream; 1 teaspoonful of soda; nutmeg, allspice and cinnamon to taste; 1 cup of blackberry jam; stir all together and bake in sheets like gingerbread, and spread with icing.

GINGER SNAPS.
Mrs. Geo. Johnson.

5 pints of sifted flour; ¼ lb. of butter; 1 pint of molasses; ½ teaspoon of soda; 1 teacup of rolled sugar; 1 tablespoonful of ginger; 1 tablespoonful of cinnamon.

MADISON CAKE.

½ lb. of butter; ¾ lb. of sugar; 1 lb. of flour; 8 eggs; 1 gill of cream, or rich milk; 1 nutmeg; ¾ lb. of raisins, seeded and chopped; ¾ lb. of currants, washed and dried; ½ lb. of citron, cut fine. Beat the butter and sugar until very light, to which add the cream; whisk the eggs very lightly, and add gradually with the flour, and spice, and, lastly, add the fruit. Line the pan with buttered paper, and bake in a moderate oven.

COFFEE CAKE.

1 cup of butter; 2 cups of sugar; 1½ cups of molasses; 1 lb. of raisins; 1½ cups of coffee, (prepared as for the table;) 1 teaspoon of soda; 2 teaspoons of cream of tartar; 8 cups of flour; 3 eggs; 1 tablespoon of cloves; 1 tablespoon of cinnamon; 1 lemon.

DELICIOUS CAKE.

1 cup of butter; 2 cups of white sugar; 1 cup of milk; 3 eggs; ½ teaspoon of soda; a scant teaspoonful of cream of tartar; 3 cups of flour. Stir butter and sugar together, then add the beaten yolks, then the beaten whites of eggs. Dissolve soda in milk, rub the cream of tartar in flour, and add the last thing.

KISSES.

Mrs. W. Van Der Lyn.

To the white of 1 egg, 9 teaspoons of granulated sugar; 1 of corn starch; beat the eggs very stiff; drop them with a teaspoon on paper that cold water has been poured over. Bake slowly in a moderate oven.

QUEEN'S CAKE.

Mrs. J. W. Clarke.

1 lb of sugar; ½ lb of butter; 5 eggs; ½ teacup of cream; 1 teaspoonful of soda; 2 teaspoonfuls of cream of tartar; 1½ teaspoonfuls of cloves; 1 teaspoonful of mace; 3 lbs of raisins; ½ lb of citron; 1 lb of flour.

CURRANT LOAF.

Mrs. Mary A. Grimes.

2 qts. of flour; 1 lb of currants; 1 large cup of sugar; 3 eggs; spice to taste; ½ lb of butter or lard; 1 gill of yeast. Knead all together when raised light. Bake in a moderate oven.

DRIED APPLE CAKE.

2 cups of dried apples, soaked one night, then chopped rather fine; add 1 cup of molasses, and let them cook a little; when

cold, add to cake 1½ cups of sugar, 3 cups of flour, ⅔ cup of butter, 1 cup of raisins, 8 teaspoonfuls of water, 1 teaspoonful of soda, a little citron and spice to taste.

LINCOLN CAKE.

1½ or 2 cups of sugar; ½ cup of butter; 2 eggs; 1 cup of sweet milk or water; 3 teaspoonfuls of baking powder, thoroughly mixed through 3 cups of flour.

CLAY CAKE.

Mrs. Hull.

1 lb of sugar; ½ lb of butter; 1 lb of flour; ½ pint of cream; 6 eggs; 2 teaspoonfuls of cream of tartar; 1 teaspoonful of soda; flavor to taste.

FEDERAL CAKE.

½ cup of butter; 2 cups of sugar; 3 cups of flour; ½ cup of sweet milk; 3 eggs; 1 teaspoonful of cream of tartar; ½ of soda; 1 lb of fruit.

MUNN CAKE.

Mrs. M. B. Ross.

2 cups of sugar; 1 cup of butter; 4 eggs; 1 cup of sweet milk; 1 teaspoonful of soda; flour enough to make it as thick as ordinary cake; 2 small cups of raisins, seeded and chopped; cinnamon and spices to your taste.

CLOVE CAKE.

Mrs. A. McFarland.

3 cups of sugar; 4 cups of flour; 1½ cups of butter; 1 cup of milk; 1 lb of raisins; 1 lb of currants; 1½ teaspoonfuls of baking powder; 1 tablespoonful of cloves; 1 tablespoonful of cinnamon; 1 nutmeg; 4 eggs.

A GOOD SUGGESTION.

In baking cake or bread, always place a bowl of water in the oven; this will prevent scorching.

CANDY.

BUTTERSCOTCH.
Mrs O. A. Lodwick.

1 pint N. O. sugar, ¼ pint of N. O. molasses, 4 tablespoonfuls of vinegar, as much pulverized alum as will lay on a knife blade, the same of baking powder, butter, (free from salt,) the size of an egg. Flavor with 4 drops of lemon.

CHOCOLATE CARAMELS.
Miss Emma T. Johnson.

3 lbs of coffee sugar, 1 lb of butter, 1 cup of cream, 1 cake of Baker's chocolate. Dissolve sugar in cream, then add butter and chocolate, and vanilla to taste.

SUGAR CANDY.
Mrs. Geo. O. Newman.

6 cups of sugar; 1 cup of vinegar; 1 cup of water; tablespoonful of butter put in at the last with 1 teaspoonful of soda dissolved in hot water; boil without stirring half an hour, or until it crisps in cold water. Pull white with the tips of your fingers.

WALNUT CANDY.
Mrs. Jas. W. Newman.

1 pt. of silver drip molasses; 1 pt. of walnut kernels; ½ pt. of coffee sugar; a piece of butter the size of a walnut, and a

small pinch of salt; stir all together in a skillet before putting on the fire; boil until brittle when dropped in water, stirring often to keep the candy from burning.

HOME-MADE CANDY.

To 1 cup of sugar, (New Orleans is best,) add 1 cup of cider vinegar; if the vinegar be very sour, put in ⅓ water. Boil fifteen to twenty minutes, then work till white.

CHOCOLATE CARAMELS.
Miss Jennie Gharky.

1 teacupful of sugar, 1 teacupful of molasses, 1 teacupful of milk, ½ teacupful of butter, ¼ pound of chocolate.

CHOCOLATE CARAMELS.
Miss Mamie Gibbs.

2 cups of sugar, 1 cup of butter, 1 cup of milk, ½ cup of grated chocolate, alum size of a pea.

CREAM CANDY.
Miss Julia Pursell.

1 qt. of white sugar, ¾ pt. of water, ¼ pt. of vinegar. Boil these until it hardens when dropped into water; then add 2 teaspoons of vanilla or lemon, butter, the size of an egg; be careful not to stir while boiling. When sufficiently cooked, pour on buttered dishes to cool; when nearly cold, pull until white.

COCOANUT DROPS.
Miss Kate Crichton.

To 1 lb of cocoanut add ½ lb of sugar, whites of 6 eggs; there should be egg enough to moisten the whole. Drop on paper and bake.

EVERTON TAFFY.

1½ lbs of brown sugar, 3 oz. of butter, 1½ teacups of water, 1 lemon. Boil the sugar, butter, water, and half the rind of a lemon together; have a quick fire, and stir it all the time; when it is quite crisp in water, set it aside until the boiling stops, then stir in the juice of the lemon. Butter a dish, and pour it in a quarter of an inch thick.

BUTTER SCOTCH.
Mrs. Geo. O. Newman.

1 pt. N. O. molasses, 1 pt. sugar, ½ pt. butter; stir all together and boil till, when dropped in cold water, it will be brittle. Pour out in well buttered pans and let cool.

REMEDIES

—AND—

FOOD FOR THE SICK.

GENERAL REMARKS.

There can be no greater accomplishment in a housekeeper than that of being able to cook nice, dainty preparations for the sick. Nothing disgusts an invalid so much as to be given food looking mussed and untidy. Let all dishes be fresh and sweet, and all food looking clean and dainty.

Be careful in making porridge or gruel, to have it free from lumps. Always mix the flour or meal in a part of the water, and stir it into the remainder.

TO CURE AGUE.

Squeeze the juice from plantain leaves, and take a tablespoonful three times a day.

FOR COUGH.

One teaspoonful of sweet spirits of nitre in half a teacup of water three times a day—midway between meals, and at bedtime.

LOCK-JAW.

A poultice of scraped beet.

BOILS.

Take beet leaves, wilt, bruise, and use as a poultice; when these can not be had, scraped beet will be almost as good.

NIGHT SWEATS.

Sage tea, drank cold, is excellent.

BOWEL COMPLAINTS.

For children or adults the following is very good, and also for infants during the second summer: 1 lb of blackberry root to 1 pt. of water; simmer slow until reduced one-half; add sugar to make a thick syrup. For a child, a teaspoonful three times a day; in bad cases, oftener.

FOR SORE BREAST.

Mutton tallow size of an egg; beeswax, half size of egg; $\frac{1}{2}$ pt. of sweet oil; 1 tablespoonful of saffron; rosin size of an egg, powdered and thoroughly melted. Add to the mixture 1 teaspoonful of spirits of camphor, and $\frac{1}{2}$ teaspoonful of turpentine.

FOR SORE BREAST.

$\frac{1}{2}$ teacup of ground allspice; $\frac{1}{2}$ teacup of white pepper; $\frac{1}{2}$

teacup of mutton tallow; ¼ teacup of beeswax; rosin as large as a walnut; 2 tablespoonfuls of honey. Heat the above well together, but do not let it burn. Dip in a linen cloth, and lay on the breast; change as often as it gets cool.

COUGH SYRUP.

Mrs. G. Lytton.

5 cts. worth of boneset; 5 cts. worth of life-everlasting; 5 cts. worth of spignet; 5 cts. worth of comfrey; 5 cts. worth of licorice; 10 cts. worth of gum arabic; 10 cts. worth of honey; ½ ℔ of white sugar; boil the roots and herbs together, strain and add the rest; boil in half-gallon of water; when done, you will have about three pints; a wine-glass full for a dose three or four times a day.

CURE FOR COUGH.

3 oz. of pure pine tree gum, dissolved in ½ pt. of alcohol, with 1 oz. of essence of juniper; when the gum is dissolved, add 1 qt. of Holland gin—gin would be dangerous except as used in this recipe; take 3 ℔s of white sugar, and add to it ½ pt. of water; boil this until it becomes a syrup; pour the other ingredients in, stir well, and strain. Dose, a tablespoonful three or four times daily.

COUGH MIXTURE.

2 quarts of rain water; 1 ℔ of raisins; 5 cts. worth of licorice; ¼ ℔ of rock candy. Boil this to 1 quart; strain; 2 tablespoonfuls three times daily; add a little vinegar when taken.

CURE FOR DROPSY.

1 pt. of strong ginger tea; 1 oz. of cream tartar; this whole quantity is to be taken daily until there is a marked improvement in the patient, after which a smaller quantity will answer.

A COLD.

A hot lemonade is one of the best remedies in the world for

cold. It acts promptly, and has no unpleasant after-effects. One lemon, properly squeezed, cut in slices, put with sugar and covered with half a pint of boiling water. Drink just before going to bed, and do not expose yourself the next day. This remedy will ward off an attack of chills and fever, if used promptly.

REMEDY FOR CROUP.

½ teaspoonful pulverized alum in a small quantity of molasses; repeat dose every hour until the patient is relieved.

DIARRHŒA.
Mrs. S. Fuller.

A tablespoonful of flour, mixed in a tumbler of water, and taken at intervals during the day, will cure diarrhœa.

CURE FOR HEADACHE.
Mrs. E. Pond.

Put a handful of salt in a quart of water; add 1 oz. of spirits of hartshorn and half an ounce of camphorated spirits of wine; put them quickly into a bottle and cork tightly, to prevent the escape of the spirits; soak a piece of rag with the mixture, and apply it to the head; wet the rag afresh as soon as it gets heated.

DRIED FLOUR FOR FEEDING CHILDREN.
M. H.

1 cup of flour, tied in a strong muslin bag and dropped into cold water; then boil three hours; turn out the flour ball and dry in the sun all day; or, if needed at once, dry in a moderate oven, without shutting the door. To use it—Grate a tablespoonful for a cup full of boiling milk and water (half and half); wet the flour with a very little cold water. Stir in and boil five minutes; add a little salt; sweeten, if you wish.

TEA LEAVES FOR BURNS.

Tea leaves, slightly steeped, cooled, and laid on a burn, will quickly relieve the pain and inflammation. They will doubtless help to do this for a minutes, at least, until flour can be applied. In all cases where the burn breaks the skin, a coat of wheat flour, put on dry, is the very best application.

CURE FOR NEURALGIA.
Mrs. T. J. Graham.

Pulverised sal. ammonia, ¼ oz.; camphor water, 3 oz.; mix. Dose, one teaspoonful 4 or 5 times a day.

SURE CURE FOR FELON.

Strong, mercurial ointment, spread on linen cloth. Apply when the sore first appears.

HERB TEAS.
Marian Harland.

Herb teas are made by infusing the dried or green leaves or stalks in boiling water, and letting them stand until cold. Sweeten to taste.

Sage tea, sweetened with honey, is good for a sore throat, used as a gargle, with a small bit of alum dissolved in it.

Catnip tea is the best panacea for infant ills, in the way of cold and colic, known to nurses.

Pennyroyal tea will often avert the unpleasant consequences of a sudden check of perspiration, or the evils induced by ladies' thin shoes.

Chamomile and gentian teas are excellent tonics, taken either cold or hot.

The tea made from blackberry roots is said to be good for summer disorders. That from green strawberry leaves is an admirable and soothing wash for a cankered mouth.

Tea of parsley root, scraped and steeped in boiling water, taken warm, will often cure strangury and kindred affections, as will that made from dried pumpkin seeds.

Tansy, rue and fennel seeds are useful in cases of colic.

A tea of damask rose leaves, dry or fresh, will usually subdue any simple case of summer complaint in infants.

Mint tea, made from the green leaves, crushed in cold or hot water, and sweetened, is palatable and healing to the stomach and bowels.

CORN MEAL GRUEL.
Mrs. C. E. Turley.

4 tablespoonfuls of meal, made into a smooth batter with cold water; pour it into a quart of water actually boiling. Continue to boil for one-half hour, stirring well from the bottom; season with salt. Some prefer it sweetened.

BEEF TEA.

1 or 2 pounds from the neck of the beef, cut in small pieces, (being careful to remove the fat;) put it into a wide-mouthed bottle, cork it, and set in a vessel partly filled with cold water, and place over the fire; let it cook slowly until the juice is extracted. Salt to taste.

TOAST WATER.

Toast 2 thin slices of bread a nice brown, put them into a quart pitcher, and fill with cold water. Cover and let stand a few minutes before it is used.

VINEGAR WHEY.

4 tablespoonfuls of good vinegar sweetened with white sugar; stir it into a pint of boiling milk; set it over the fire and let it simmer ten minutes; strain it through a fine sieve. When cold, if not sufficiently sweet, add sugar.

MULLED EGG.

1 egg, well beaten, 1 slice of bread, toasted, broken into small bits; over this pour a pint of boiling water, stirring all the while. Sweeten to taste. Nutmeg.

CREAM NECTAR.

Put 2 lbs of sugar and 2 oz. of tartaric acid in 3 pts of water;

set on the stove and boil about five minutes, then set it away to cool; beat the whites of four eggs to a very stiff froth, then beat in ½ cup of flour and the juice of two lemons; stir this in the liquid, and add 1 tablespoonful of the essence of wintergreen. Bottle and keep in a cool place. Put 2 tablespoonfuls of syrup in a tumbler, fill it ⅔ full of water, add a very little soda. Stir it up.

CHICKEN BROTH.
Mrs. C. E. Turley.

Cut the chicken small and crack the bones well; put it into 1 qt. of cold water, without salt; cook until it falls to pieces; strain, add 1 tablespoonful of rice or barley, soaked in a very little warm water; 4 tablespoonfuls of milk; salt and pepper; simmer for five minutes, taking care it does not burn. Serve hot with crackers.

RASPBERRY SHRUB.

Put raspberries into a pan and scarcely cover them with strong vinegar; add 1 pt. of sugar to 1 pt. of juice. Scald it, skim it, and bottle when cool.

DRINK FOR SICK.

1 oz. of gum arabic in a large glass, a lump of ice, and fill with water.

RICE JELLY.

Boil ¼ ℔ rice flour with ½ ℔ of loaf sugar in 1 qt. of water until it becomes one mass. Strain off the jelly and let it cool.

BLACKBERRY CORDIAL.

To 1 pt. of juice add 1 ℔ of sugar; boil twenty-five minutes; add cinnamon and cloves to your taste. Seal while hot.

SAGO GRUEL.

2½ cups of water, 2 tablespoonfuls of sago, 3 teaspoonfuls of white sugar, 1 tablespoonful of lemon juice or nutmeg to taste, and a pinch of salt.

OYSTER TOAST.

To 6 oysters take ½ teacup of their own liquor, the same of milk; boil one minute. Season with butter, pepper and salt, and pour over a slice of buttered toast.

BEEF TEA.
Mrs. C. E. Turley.

1 lb of lean beef cut in small pieces; put in a jar without a drop of water, cover tightly and set into a pot of cold water; heat gradually to a boil, and continue boiling steadily for three or four hours, until the juice is all drawn out; season with salt, and when cold, skim. The patient will often prefer this ice cold.

CORN MEAL GRUEL.

2 qts. of boiling water, 1 cup of meal, 1 tablespoonful of flour; salt to taste, or use sugar and nutmeg. Wet the meal and flour to a smooth paste with cold water; stir into the water while it is boiling. Boil slowly half an hour, keeping it well stirred to prevent burning.

EGG AND MILK.

Beat separately the yolk and white of a fresh egg, sweeten it to your taste, and add to the yolk a tumbler of fresh milk, then stir in the white.

OAT MEAL GRUEL.

Mix two tablespoonfuls of oat meal with a little cold water, and stir it into a pt. of boiling water and let it boil fifteen minutes; add a little salt or sugar, to taste, also a little nutmeg, if approved.

PAP OF BOILED FLOUR.

Tie a teacupful of flour closely in a cloth and boil it six hours, then grate some of it and mix with cold milk until of the consistency of thin starch, then stir into boiling milk; when done, sweeten to taste with loaf sugar; salt can be used to season, if preferred.

SHERBET.

Make 1 qt. of strong lemonade, add 1 qt. of milk, and then freeze.

SMITH'S COUGH POWDER.
Mrs. Currie.

Elecampane root, 2 oz., licorice, 2 oz., blood root, 2 oz., crane's-bill, 2 oz., Indian turnip, 2 oz., all pulverized fine. Dose—$\frac{1}{2}$ teaspoonful three times daily. This is a good expectorant, pectoral and tonic.

CURE FOR FELON.

As soon as inflammation begins, take tincture of lobelia, saturate a cloth and bind it on. This will kill the felon.

PLASTER FOR GATHERED BREAST.
Mrs. A. Reed.

$\frac{1}{2}$ teacupful of allspice, $\frac{1}{2}$ teacupful of black pepper, $\frac{1}{2}$ teacup of mutton tallow, $\frac{1}{4}$ teacup of beeswax, rosin as large as a walnut, 2 tablespoonfuls of honey.

TO AVOID A COLD.

Change the stockings two or three times a day, if they become wet from perspiration. Avoid cold draughts upon any part of the body; or unequal temperature from any cause, such as evaporation of moisture from wet clothes on a portion of the person. The clothing wet all over, is less productive of colds than when partly wet. You might jump naked into a snow bank and not take cold, but receive serious injury from immersing only a hand or a foot in the snow, while the rest of the body is kept warm. Unequal temperature upon different parts of the body, disturbs the circulation of the blood and produces a cold. The best precaution, however, is to keep the system vigorous by temperance, by a generous diet of digestible food, with plenty of sleep.

ANTI-CHOLERA MIXTURE.
Mrs. Currie.

1½ drachm tincture of ammonia, 1½ drachm of camphor, 1¼ drachm of opium, ½ drachm of rhubarb, 1½ drachm of cayenne pepper, 1½ drachm of essence of peppermint. Dose—15 drops every fifteen minutes, in a wine glass of water, until checked.

FOR FROZEN FLESH.

A poultice made of corn meal, mixed with an infusion of young hyson tea, and laid over burns and frozen flesh as hot as can be borne, will relieve pain.

POTATO POULTICE.

Potato poultice, more agreeable than bread, keeps heat longer; can be re-heated. Peel, boil, mash fine, spread on a cloth, moisten and apply.

CURE FOR DYSPEPSIA.

Mix together equal quantities of bran and sugar, and brown in the oven like coffee; take two or three times a day.

FOR CORNS.

The strongest acetic acid, applied night and morning, will remove hard or soft corns in a week.

TO PREVENT WOUNDS FROM MORTIFYING.

Sprinkle sugar on them. Obstinate ulcers may be cured with sugar dissolved in a strong decoction of walnut leaves.

CURE FOR WASP STINGS.

Flour mixed with saleratus water and made into a poultice. Raw onions sliced for a bee sting.

HOP POULTICE.

A handful of hops boiled in a pint of water, and mixed with corn meal, is good for a sore throat or swelled face.

MUSTARD PLASTER.

To make mustard plaster, use whites of eggs, and it will not blister.

SALVE.
Mrs. T. G. Lloyd.

1 oz. vial of Venice turpentine; 1 oz. of rosin; ½ lb of butter (without salt); 1 oz. of red precipitate. Pulverize the rosin and sift it through book muslin; rub the butter with your hands until it creams, and lastly mix in turpentine and red precipitate.

TO CURE A WEN.

Wash it with common salt, dissolved in water, every day, and it will be removed in a short time.

TO CURE DIPTHERIA.
Mrs. E. Pond.

Take a common tobacco pipe, place a live coal in the bowl, drop a little tar on the coal, draw the smoke into the mouth, and discharge it through the nostrils.

TO PREVENT FLIES INJURING PICTURE FRAMES

Boil three or four onions in one pint of water; brush your frames over with the liquid, and no fly will touch them. It will not injure your frames.

TO CURE WHITE SWELLING ON THE KNEE.

A poultice of elder leaves applied around the knee, and changed three times a day. This has been tried when amputation seemed necessary, and proved a cure.

TO PREVENT A FELON.
Mrs. E. Pond.

When a soreness is felt, immerse the fingers in a basin of wood ashes and cold water; set it on the stove while cold and stir it continually without taking it out, till the lye is so hot it cannot be borne any longer; if the soreness is not gone in half an hour, repeat it.

SIMPLE REMEDY FOR RHEUMATISM.

Bathe the parts affected with hot potato water.

CURE FOR STRAIN.
Miss E. Bell.

The yolk of 1 egg and salt to mix to a salve.

ROCK CANDY COUGH MIXTURE.
Mrs. A. P.

½ lb. rock candy; 2 oz. of best gum arabic; 3 lemons (juice only); ½ pt. of water; steam until dissolved; desertspoonful a dose.

A SPEEDY REMEDY FOR CROUP.
Mrs. Wm. Armstrong, Ripley, O.

1 tablespoonful of melted lard, taken inwardly; saturate a piece of cloth with lard not melted, cover thick with grated nutmeg, then lay it on the throat and chest.

TOOTHACHE REMEDY.

A roasted onion bound on the wrist, over the pulse, will stop the ache in a few minutes.

CURE FOR PHTHISIC AND ASTHMA.
Mrs. Wm. Armstrong, Ripley, O.

1 teaspoonful of white mustard seed, taken whenever the symptoms are felt. It will arrest it instantly. [This is also good for a cough; dose, 1 teaspoonful, three times a day.—Mrs. Fuller.]

CURE FOR SCURVY OR CANKER SORE MOUTH.

Burn a corn cob, and use the ashes. Apply to the sore three or four times a day.

CURE FOR HOARSENESS.

Whites of 2 eggs, beat with 2 spoonfuls of white sugar; nutmeg; 1 pt. of warm water; stir well, and drink often.

MISCELLANEOUS.

HARD SOAP.
Mrs. A. McFarland.

Pour four gallons of boiling water over six pounds of sal soda and three pounds of unslacked lime. Stir it so as to get the strength; let it stand over night; pour the liquor off carefully, add six lbs of soap fat, and boil until it becomes thick like honey. Stir it occasionally, and add a handful of salt just before taking it off from the fire.

EXCELLENT HAIR WASH.

Take one ounce of borax, half an ounce of camphor; powder these ingredients fine, and dissolve them in one quart of boiling water; when cool, the solution will be ready for use; dampen the hair frequently. This wash effectually cleanses, beautifies, and strengthens the hair, preserves the color, and prevents early baldness. The camphor will form into lumps after being dissolved, but the water will be sufficiently impregnated.

TO TAKE OUT GREASE.
Mrs. A. McFarland.

To erase sewing machine oil from muslins, soap the spots and wash in cold water.

A CLEANING POLISH FOR FURNITURE.

Take of olive oil 1 pound. of rectified oil of amber, 1 pound; spirits of turpentine, 1 lb.; oil of lavender, 1 oz.; tincture of alkanet root, $\frac{1}{2}$ oz. Saturate a piece of cotton batting with this, and apply it to the wood, then with a soft rag, rub well and wipe off dry. This will make old things new. Must be kept tightly corked.

TO RESTORE GILT FRAMES.
Mrs. D. McFarland.

Take one ounce of cooking soda and beat it thoroughly with the whites of three eggs. Blow off the dust with a pair of bellows, or brush it out with a feather duster, then dip a small paint brush into the mixture, and rub it all over the gilding, into every tiny crevice, and it will render it fresh and bright.

COLD WATER SOAP.
Mrs. N. Barker.

14 lbs. of rosin bar soap; 3 lbs. of sal soda; 1 lb. of rosin; 8 oz. of salt; put these in 6 or 7 gallons of soft water on the fire till dissolved, then put the same in a barrel and fill with soft water; add 2 oz. of spirits of turpentine and stir well.

TO CLEAN SILVER.

$\frac{1}{2}$ lb of cyanide of potassium; $\frac{1}{2}$ lb of salts of tartar. Dissolve this in 1 gallon of soft water. Put the article to be cleaned in the solution a minute or two, then wash in hot soap suds, and rub with soft cloth. This solution must be used in an earthen vessel when cleaning silver, as it is poisonous. The same solution can be rebottled and used many times.

FOR DISOBEDIENT CHILDREN.
Mrs. C. E. Turley.

Take a nice, green, limber switch, from a thrifty young peach tree; apply briskly where the clothes are thickest. Amen.

TO DESTROY FLIES.
Mrs. A. McFarland.

Strong tea sweetened well and set in saucers, will attract flies, and destroy them as effectually as the poisoned paper commonly used.

TO CLEAN CARPETS.

Salt, sprinkled upon the carpet before sweeping, will make it look bright and clean. This will also prevent moths.

WASHING FLUID.

1 lb. of sal soda; 1 lb. of lime, over which pour 2 gallons of boiling water; let it stand until settled. Strain, and add 10 oz. of brown soap, sliced up. Let it simmer until dissolved, then put in stone or glass vessels and cork tight.

DEATH TO INSECTS.

2 lbs of alum dissolved in three or four quarts of boiling water, and applied to all cracks and crevices, will keep out ants, roaches, spiders, bedbugs, &c., &c.

TO REMOVE WATER STAINS FROM BLACK CRAPE.

When a drop of water falls on a black crape veil or collar, it is apt to leave a white spot, which may be removed by spreading the crape on a table, having a piece of old black silk underneath, and taking a camel's hair brush, dipped in common black ink and rubbing over the spot, then wipe the ink off with a piece of silk. It will dry immediately, and the spot will have disappeared.

DEATH TO BEDBUGS ESPECIALLY.

$\frac{1}{4}$ lb. of fish berries, cracked; 1 pint of water; boil these together until reduced to $\frac{1}{2}$ pint; add 1 pint of whisky, bottle and mark poison. Apply with brush.

TO SET THE COLORS OF CALICOES.

One oz. of sugar of lead to a gallon of water will set the colors of two dresses.

CAMPHOR ICE.

1 oz. of white wax; 2 oz. of spermaceti; 1 oz. of gum of camphor; 1 oz. of olive oil; melt slowly on stove. Put up air tight.

TO CLEAN WHITE PAINT.

A tablespoonful of ammonia to a quart of water. Wash with a soft cloth.

TO CLEAN BRASS STAIR RODS.

Mix coal oil with ashes, and scour well, then rub off with dry ashes.

TO REMOVE PIMPLES AND MAKE THE SKIN SMOOTH.

Make a tea of red clover blossoms, and wash the face two or three times daily.

SOFT SOAP.

Mrs. Currie.

20 lbs of strained grease; 18 lbs. of potash; 2 lbs. of rosin; turn in grease first, then the rosin; dissolve potash in hot water, stir it vigorously. After it has had time to purify itself by set-

tling, turn in the solution on the grease, stir it again, and add sufficient water to make a barrel of soap. Repeat the stirring every day for a week.

TO CLEAN CARPETS.

Shake them well and tack them down, then mix half a pint of bullock's gall with 2 gallons of soft water; use soap and this mixture; scrub with a soft brush; rub dry. Your carpet will look like new.

TO CLEAN STRAW MATTING.

A coarse cloth dipped in salt and water; wipe dry. The salt will keep the matting from turning yellow.

SALVE FOR CHAPPED LIPS AND HANDS.
Mrs. E. Pond.

Take 2 oz. of white wax, 1 oz. of spermaceti, 4 oz. of oil of almond, 2 oz. of English honey, ¼ oz. essence of bergamot, or any other scent. Melt the wax and spermaceti, then add the honey and melt all together, and when hot, add the almond oil by degrees, stirring till cold.

TO POLISH FURNITURE.

One part of flaxseed oil; three parts of alcohol; shake well and apply with silk or linen cloth, then rub hard and dry with another cloth, or chamois skin.

TO REMOVE ODOR.

To remove the disagreeable odor within a refrigerator, apply gum shellac two or three times to all the wood work exposed in the inside, being particular to have the wood perfectly dry before the first application. The gum shellac can be purchased at any paint shop, and costs but a trifle. It closes all the pores of the wood, thus stopping absorption, which is the cause of the musty odor.

TO REMOVE RUST FROM STEEL.

Rub with sweet oil; after two days, clean with pulverized lime.

TO TAKE GREASE OUT OF SILKS.
Mrs. Graham.

Take a lump of magnesia and rub it, (wet,) over the spot, let it dry, then brush the powder off, and the spot will disappear. Or take a visiting, or other card, separate it and rub the spot with the soft internal part, and it will disappear without taking the gloss off the silk.

TO EXTERMINATE ROACHES.
Mrs. A. McFarland.

Procure a small quantity of Paris green from the druggist, and put it into a small tin box with perforated top. Sift it in the corners and places infested with roaches, and it will exterminate them in a very short time. As the Paris green is poison the box should be marked "poison."

TOOTH POWDER.
Mrs. T. J. Graham.

Pulverized orris root, 2 oz.; English prepared chalk, 2 oz.; cuttle fish bone, scraped, 1 oz.; pulverized gum myrrh, $\frac{1}{4}$ oz.; pulverized white sugar, 1 oz. Scent with otto of roses.

PEARL DROPS FOR THE SKIN.
Mrs. Emma L. Kendall.

1 lb. of flake white; $\frac{1}{2}$ pint of bay rum; 3 pints of rain water; $\frac{1}{2}$ oz. of glycerine, and a few drops of oil of rose; a few drops of vinegar rouge. Boil the water and pour over the flake white, and stir well until smooth.

TO DESTROY FLIES.

To destroy flies in a room, take half a teaspoonful of black pepper in powder, one teaspoonful of brown sugar, and one tablespoonful of cream; mix them well together, and place them in a room on a plate, where the flies are troublesome, and they will soon disappear.

RASPBERRY VINEGAR.
M. F.

Put a quart of fine fruit into a bowl, and pour upon it a quart of the best vinegar; next day strain the liquor, and squeeze the fruit on a quart of fresh raspberries, and the following day do the same; the last time, pass it through a canvas bag previously wet' with vinegar, to prevent waste. Put it into a stone jar, with a pound of white sugar to every pint of juice, then put the jar into a kettle of water; let it simmer; skim it, and when cold, bottle it.

TO PRESERVE POTATOES TILL SPRING.

Put a quantity of powdered charcoal on the bottom of the potato bin; it will preserve their flavor, and prevent the sprouts from shooting out so early as they otherwise would.

TO MAKE AN OLD FOWL TENDER.
L. E. W.

1 tablespoonful of lemon juice put in the water in which it is boiled. Strong vinegar may be used, but is not so good.

FINE COLOGNE WATER.
Mrs. C. E. Turley.

1 drachm of oil of bergamot; 1 drachm of oil of lavender; 2 drachms of oil of lemon; 2 drachms of oil of rosemary; 50 drops of tincture of musk; 8 drops of oil of cinnamon; 8 drops of oil of cloves; 1 pint of alcohol.

LEMON ICE.
Mrs. John G. Peebles.

1 lb. of sugar to a quart of water; let it dissolve; 3 large lem-

ons. Just before you put it in the freezer, add the whites of 2 well beaten eggs. This will make one quart. Increase in proportion.

ICE (COUNTERFEIT PURE) CREAM.
Mrs. C. E. T.

To 2 qts. of milk, add the yolks of 8 eggs, well beaten, and two jelly cups of sugar; heat almost to boiling, then add 1 tablespoonful of flour (made into a smooth batter with cold milk,) and the white of eggs beaten to a stiff froth; heat until it thickens, stirring constantly. Set aside until cool. Flavor and freeze.

RASPBERRY VINEGAR.
Mrs. J. N. Stanger.

Cover your raspberries with vinegar and let them stand a week. To every pint, when strained, add a teacup of water and $2\frac{1}{2}$ lbs. of sugar, and boil five minutes.

COTTAGE CHEESE.

Take one or more quarts of sour milk, put it in a warm place, and let it remain until the whey separates from the curd, then pour it into a bag and hang it up; let it drain until all the whey has dripped from it, then turn it out, and mash with a spoon until very fine; add cream, with salt to taste, before sending to table. A little nutmeg added, makes it very palatable for some.

HOW TO KEEP MEAT.

Meat may be kept several days in the height of summer, sweet and good, by lightly covering it with bran, and hanging it in a room where there is a current of air.

TO SWEETEN CASKS.

$\frac{1}{2}$ pint of vitrol mixed with a quart of water, and the mixture poured into the barrel, roll about; next day, add 1 lb of chalk, and roll again. Bung down two or three days, then rinse well with hot water.

TO EXTINGUISH A FIRE IN A CHIMNEY.

Throw some powdered brimstone on the fire in the grate, then put a board or something in front of the fire place. The vapor of the brimstone ascending the chimney, will extinguish the soot on fire.

TO CLEAN MIRRORS.

Wash the glass with soapsuds and a sponge. When dry, rub it with a buckskin and a little prepared chalk, finely powdered.

SCENT BAGS.

Lavender flowers, ½ lb; rose leaves, ½ lb; dried thyme and mint, of each, ½ oz.; ground cloves and caraways, of each, ¼ oz.; common salt, dried, 1 oz. Mix the whole well together, and put in silk or cambric bags. It will perfume the drawer and linen nicely.

TO PURIFY GLASS VESSELS.

Glass vessels, and other utensils may be purified and cleaned, by rinsing them out with powdered charcoal.

ROSE HAIR OIL.

1 pint of olive oil; 15 to 16 drops of the otto of roses. To color it red, use alkanet root, 1 drachm.

FURNITURE POLISH.

Dissolve one ounce of Venice turpentine in half a pint of alcohol.

POISONS AND THEIR ANTIDOTES.

MURIATIC ACID (SPIRITS OF SALT.)—Mix an ounce of calcined magnesia with a quart of water, and give a wineglassful every five minutes. Soap, chalk, or whiting scraped off the wall, mixed with water, milk, oil, white of eggs, or demulcents of any kind, may be given till magnesia can be obtained. Vomiting to be afterward excited by tickling the throat with a feather or the finger.

SULPHURIC ACID (OIL OF VITRIOL.)—The antidotes to this poison, are calcined magnesia or the carbonate of magnesia, finely powdered, and mixed with milk or water as above. These should be administered immediately. In the absence of these, give soapsuds, water of wood ashes, milk, sweet oil, gruel, or any mild diluent that first comes at hand, and do not lose a moment in waiting for the most appropriate chemical remedy. External parts, burnt with the acid, should be washed with soap and water.

NITRIC ACID (AQUA FORTIS.)—The antidotes are the same as for sulphuric acid.

PRUSSIC ACID, OR SUBSTANCES CONTAINING IT, AS OIL OF BITTER ALMONDS, CHERRY-LAUREL WATER, WILD CHERRIES, &C.—A stream of cold water, as cold as can be obtained, should be poured from a pitcher, on the head and spine, and also dashed upon the face and chest. The only antidote known that can be conveniently resorted to, is ammonia, which should be administered as soon as possible. If hartshorn is not at hand, give ten or twelve grains of the salts out of a common smelling-bottle, and apply it at the same time to the nostrils.

OXALIC ACID.—Give an emetic, and favor copious vomiting by plenty of warm water, and then proceed as in poisoning from muriatic or sulphuric acid.

ACONITE.—If vomiting has not been occasioned by the poison, it should be excited at once by some active emetic, and favored as much as possible by tepid drinks or gruel. A cup of very strong coffee, or vinegar, diluted with water, may then be given with advantage. If there be insensibility, friction and warm mustard pastes or blisters should be resorted to.

POTASH.—Give vinegar diluted with water, lemon juice, milk, oil, mucilaginous drinks, and induce free vomiting.

AMMONIA.—Give the same remedies as in poisoning by potash.

BELLADONNA.—Stomach-pump, or an active emetic as soon as possible.

HELLEBORE.—Same as for belladonna.

CALOMEL.—Give whites of eggs, milk, sweet, sperm or castor oil, flour beaten up with water, gruel, etc., until a stomach pump can be obtained.

CANTHARIDES (SPANISH FLY.)—An emetic, followed by mucilaginous drinks.

COPPERAS.—Same as for calomel.

VERDIGRIS.—Same as for calomel.

ARSENIC.—An emetic immediately, and vomiting to be promoted by draughts of demulcent drinks, as milk, gruel, flour and water, broths, etc. There is no antidote to be relied upon as a specific against this poison. Olive oil is extolled by some as acting to envelop the particles of arsenic, and preventing its absorption. It may be given when convenient at hand.

SUGAR OF LEAD.—Give Epsom salts dissolved in water, and incite free vomiting.

CORROSIVE SUBLIMATE (BEDBUG POISON.)—The antidotes for this poison, are the same as for calomel.

OPIUM, LAUDANUM, MORPHINE, ETC.—Give an emetic of mustard and alum, promote copious emeses, and follow with draughts of very strong coffee or diluted vinegar. Also dash cold water upon the face, and prevent the patient from sleeping by walking him around, pricking with a pin, etc.

LIME, OR LIME WATER.—Give vinegar, lemon juice, or any vegetable acid, and follow with demulcent drinks.

PHOSPHORUS.—Give large draughts of water, milk, or gruel, so as to envelope the phosphorus, and exclude it from the air contained in the alimentary canal. Then give magnesia or chalk to neutralize the poison. Oily or fatty substances should not be used. Burns occasioned by this substance, should be washed by some alkaline solution, as soda, and afterward, poulticed.

NITRATE OF SILVER.—The antidote to this poison is common table salt. Dissolve a tablespoon of this in a bowl of water, and let the patient drink of it every few minutes. Mucilaginous drinks should then be administered, followed by a dose of castor oil.

STRYCHNINE.—Give freely of whites of eggs, sweet oil, etc., and produce vomiting as soon as possible. There is no real antidote known.

PIECES OF GLASS OR POWDERED METAL.—Give large quantities of crumbs of bread to envelope the particles, and then an emetic of mustard.

IODINE.—In case of an overdose of any of the preparations of this substance being taken, the first object is to evacuate the stomach, promoting the vomiting by large draughts of demulcent liquids, especially those containing starch, as common starch of wheaten flour, sago, milk, arrowroot, etc. These to be followed by opiates.

SALTPETRE.—As there is no chemical antidote for this salt known, it should be cleared from the stomach as speedily as possible, and the patient to drink freely of milk, gum-water, or other bland mucilaginous drinks.

THE YOUNG LADY'S TOILETTE.

SELF-KNOWLEDGE—THE ENCHANTING MIRROR.

This curious glass will bring your faults to light,
And make your virtues shine both strong and bright.

CONTENTMENT—WASH TO SMOOTH WRINKLES.

A daily portion of this essence use,
'T will smooth the brow, tranquility infuse.

TRUTH—FINE LIP SALVE.

Use daily for your lips this precious dye,
They'll redden, and breathe sweet melody.

PRAYER—MIXTURE, GIVING SWEETNESS TO THE VOICE.

At morning, noon, and night, this mixture take,
Your tones improved, will richer music make.

VALUABLE RECIPES.

COMPASSION—BEST EYE WATER.

These drops will add great lustre to the eye;
When more you need, the poor will you supply.

WISDOM—SOLUTIONS TO PREVENT ERUPTIONS.

It calms the temper, beautifies the face,
And gives to woman dignity and grace.

ATTENTION AND OBEDIENCE—MATCHLESS PAIR OF EAR-RINGS.

With these clear drops appended to the ear,
Attentive lessons you will gladly hear.

NEATNESS AND INDUSTRY—INDISPENSABLE PAIR OF BRACELETS.

Clasp them on carefully each day you live,
To good designs they efficacy give.

PATIENCE—AN ELASTIC GIRDLE.

The more you use the brighter it will grow,
Though its least merit is external show.

PRINCIPLE—RING OF TRIED GOLD.

Yield not this golden circlet while you live,
'Twill sin restrain, and peace of conscience give.

RESIGNATION—NECKLACE OF PUREST PEARL.

This ornament embellishes the fair,
And teaches all the ills of life to bear.

LOVE—DIAMOND BREAST PIN.

Adorn your bosom with this precious pin;
It shines without, and warms the heart within.

POLITENESS—A GRACEFUL BANDEAU.

The forehead neatly circled with this band,
Will admiration and respect command.

PIETY—A PRECIOUS DIADEM.

Who e'er this precious diadem shall own,
Secures herself an everlasting crown.

GOOD TEMPER—UNIVERSAL BEAUTIFIER.

With this choice liquid gently touch the mouth;
It spreads o'er all the face the charms of youth.

Good Salesmen Wanted!
APPLY TO
J. T. GRAYSON.

EXAMINE THE MERITS

OF THE

NEW

Wheeler & Wilson Sewing Machine,

Before you buy any other. It is the best and the Cheapest. Over **800,000** of these Machines are now in use. 40,000 more sold annually for family use, than of any other make.

THE NEW FEED AND IMPROVEMENTS put on the old Wheeler & Wilson, and warranted as good as new. **John Clark jr. & Co's** Spool Cotton on Black Spools, is the best thread for Hand and Machine Sewing. Merchants and Dealers supplied at the

LOWEST MARKET PRICES.

A full stock always on hand. Orders from Merchants and Dealers solicited, and orders filled with dispatch. Office and Salesroom

CORNER OF WASHINGTON & 2D ST., PORTSMOUTH, O.

J. T. GRAYSON, Agent.

Sewing Machine Sales of 1873

The Singer Manufacturing Company sold............232,444
Wheeler and Wilson Manufacturing Company sold......119,190
Domestic Sewing Machine Company sold 40,114
Grover & Baker Sewing Machine Company sold.......... 36,179
Weed Sewing Machine Company sold................... 21,769
Wilson Sewing Machine Company sold.................. 21,247
Howe Machine Company sold..... ....no returns

The sales of fourteen other small companies ranged from 16,431 down to 217 machines each. While the Singer Manufacturing Company shows a

HEALTHY INCREASE

In their business over that of 1872. All other companies have fallen off largely. A glance at the above will practically demonstrate the

Superiority of the "Singer" Machine.

GEORGE D. SELBY
General Agent Singer's Machine, 119 West Second Street.

P. S. IAMS,   JAS. Y. GORDON,   WM. M. PURSELL,
President.   Cashier.   Ass't Cashier.

CAPITAL, · · $250,000.
FIRST NATIONAL BANK
OF PORTSMOUTH,
PORTSMOUTH, OHIO.

Designated Depository of the United States.

DIRECTORS,

P. S. IAMS,   L. C. DAMARIN,   B. B. GAYLORD,
JOHN P. TERRY,   JAS. Y. GORDON.

E. MILLER,

—— DEALER IN ——

CLOTHS, CASSIMERES, VESTINGS,

—— ALSO ——

Overcoatings, Shirts, Drawers, Cravats,

And all kinds of

READY-MADE CLOTHING,

Second Street, between Market and Court,

PORTSMOUTH, OHIO.

The clothing is of his own manufacture, and from the best New York houses, and will be warranted to give satisfaction.

His goods are of the finest quality, and the largest variety in the city; and his facilities will enable him to fill all orders on the shortest notice.

JAS. M. RUMSEY.   THOS. E. TYNES.   GEO. A. RUMSEY, Special.

J. M. RUMSEY & CO.,

WHOLESALE

Dry Goods & Notions,

123 West Second Street,

PORTSMOUTH, OHIO.

We sell in competition with all points, always have on hand fresh and desirable stocks of

DRY GOODS AND NOTIONS,

And cordially invite an examination of the same before purchasing elsewhere.

ADVERTISEMENTS. 155

J. H. WAIT & SON,

MANUFACTURERS OF

ALL KINDS OF FURNITURE,

WHOLESALE AND RETAIL.

Portsmouth, Ohio.

Salesroom 121 West Second Street, Factory, corner of Second and Jefferson Streets.

J. B. Nichols & Co.,

WHOLESALE

Furniture Manufacturers,

Corner of Third and Market Streets.

Buyers visiting the city are invited to call. Estimates for work furnished. Prices low as the lowest.

Cabinet Makers' Union

Wholesale Manufacturers of all kinds of

FURNITURE AND CHAIRS,

OFFICE AND SALESROOM:

205 AND 207 MARKET ST., AND 149 WEST SECOND ST.,

Factory, Mill Street, between Gay and Bond.

PORTSMOUTH, OHIO.

HIBBS, ANGLE & CO.

Dealers in

General Hardware,

135 West Front Street,

Portsmouth, O.

We have constantly in stock the following specialties, viz: Egg beaters, (several varieties), cherry seeders, apple pearers, brass kettles, spoons, table cutlery, scissors, shears, coffee mills, wood and tin sieves, brushes, pruning tools, fluting machines, (three kinds)

Mrs. Pott's Cold Handle Sad Irons,

Scales, butcher knives, lawn mowers, etc., etc.

ALBERT KNITTEL,

Baker and Confectioner,

Fancy Cake and Ice Cream.

Parties and Weddings Supplied.

Corner 4th and Court Sts., Portsmouth, O.

PETER BRODBECK,

Dealer in

DRY GOODS,

CARPETS, OIL CLOTH AND CARPET CHAIN,

Boots and Shoes, and Notions of all Kinds.

114 W. 2d St., bet. Market and Court. PORTSMOUTH, O.

House Established:
1855,
JAMES CONNOLLEY.
1860,
J. CONNOLLEY & SON.
1868,
W. A. CONNOLLEY.

Dry Goods, Notions,
Boots, Shoes,
Hats, Furs.

Stock Unrivaled for Extent, Variety, and General Adaptation to the Wants of the Retail Trade.

MOTTO---"Good Trade and Fair Treatment."

421 and 423 Chillicothe Street - - - PORTSMOUTH, O.

Ph. ZOELLNER,

Dealer in

Watches, Clocks, Jewelry and Fancy Goods,

2d St., two doors above Market, PORTSMOUTH, O.

Repairing Done Promptly, and Warranted.

Agent for

Howard & Co.'s Watches and Clocks.

MILLER, VOORHEIS & CO.,
Wholesale Clothiers,
117 WEST 2d ST., PORTSMOUTH, OHIO.

SPECIALTIES:
Piece Goods, for Men's and Boy's Wear,
JEANS, COTTONADES, ETC.
Largest Stock in This Market.

J. N. LEEDOM,
Dealer in

Dry Goods, Carpets, Oil Cloths, Boots, Shoes, Etc.

Chillicothe Street, Between 6th and 7th.

No Credit Given. Don't Ask it.

C. P. TRACY & CO.,

Manufacturers and Exclusively Wholesale Dealers in

Boots, Shoes, Hats, Leather and Findings,

131 W. Front St., PORTSMOUTH, OHIO.

Particular attention is invited to our

CUSTOM WORK!

Made at the

Portsmouth Shoe Manufactory.

DAN'L R. SPRY,

Druggist and Apothecary,

Corner Second and Market, (Fountain Place)

PORTSMOUTH, O.

DEALER IN

Drugs, Medicines, Pure Oils, Paints, Varnishes,

Fine Toilet Soaps, Brushes, Perfumery,
and Fancy Goods.

Saratoga Spring Water!
Soda from Glass Fountains!

Prescriptions and Family Compounds carefully prepared. Pure Wines and Liquors for Medicinal purposes. Dye Wood and Dye Stuff generally.

PURE GOODS AND LOW PRICES.

J. L. HIBBS.　　　　　　　　　　　　　　　　　I. N. CLOSMAN.

J. L. HIBBS & CO.,

(Late Hibbs & Co.)

Wholesale Dealers in

HARDWARE,

At the Old Stand, Sign of the Anvil,

115 and 117 W. Front St., PORTSMOUTH, OHIO.

HIBBS, RICHARDSON & CO.,

Exclusively Wholesale Dealers in

Boots, Shoes, and Hats,

116 W. 2d St., PORTSMOUTH, OHIO.

… ADVERTISEMENTS. …

PURSELL, EWING & CO.

IMPORTERS AND DEALERS IN

QUEENSWARE, GLASSWARE, CHINA, SILVER PLATED WARE, FANCY GOODS AND TOYS.

No. 125 Front Street, Portsmouth, Ohio.

Aside from a full assortment of all kinds of Queensware, China and Glassware, may be found at our house such goods as are enumerated in the following Housekeeper's List:

- Argand Burners,
- Artificial Flowers,
- Basting Spoons,
- Bronze Ornaments,
- Bread Knives,
- Butcher Knives,
- Burners,
- Biscuit Pans,
- Butter Knives,
- Baskets, Clothes,
- Baskets, Market,
- Baskets, Traveling,
- Baskets, Moss,
- Baskets, Work,
- Baskets, Lunch,
- Bracket Lamps,
- Bird Cage Hooks,
- Basins, Tin,
- Basins, Papier Mache,
- Brackets,
- Busts,
- Bath Tubs,
- Berry Bowls,
- Bureau Sets,
- Boot Jacks,
- Cake Pans,
- Cullenders,
- Chamois Skins,
- Coffee Pots,
- Coffee Pot Stands,
- Coolers,
- Carvers and Forks,
- Chandeliers,
- Chimneys,
- Coffee Mills,
- Call Bells,
- Candlesticks,
- Can Openers,
- Coal Vases,
- Casters,
- Cake Baskets,
- Chafing Dishes,
- Card Stands,
- Cake Boxes,
- Canisters,
- Chimney Cleaners,
- Childrens' Trays,
- Cologne Sets,
- Crumb Brushes,
- Crumb Pans,
- Curtain Pins,
- Cake Cutters,
- Cracker Boxes,
- Cake Pans,
- Corn Poppers,
- Dish Pans,
- Dippers,
- Dredges,
- Dusters,
- Egg Beaters,
- Foot Scrapers,
- Fruit Jars,
- Fruit Knives,
- Fruit Baskets,
- Freezers,
- Flower Pots,
- Fish Globes,
- Folding Hat Racks,
- Fruit Can Cement,
- Gas Stoves,
- Gas Shades,
- Gas Tubing,
- Gas Lighters,
- Gas Portables,
- Gas Burners,
- Graters,
- Glass Shades and Stands,
- Garden Vases,
- Gravy Ladles,
- Iced Glassware,
- Ice Chests,
- Jelly Cake Pans,
- Jelly Moulds,
- Japanese Waiters,
- Knives and Forks,
- Knives, Ivory Handle,
- Knives, Silver Plated,
- Lamps,
- Lanterns,
- Lamp Shears,
- Lamp Mats,
- Lamp Shades,
- Looking Glasses,
- Lemon Squeezers,
- Lemonade Mixers,
- Match Safes,
- Mountain Cake Pans,
- Mouse Traps,
- Milk Pans,
- Myer's Hat Racks,
- Nut Cracks,
- Napkin Rings,
- Nursery Lamps,
- Nest Eggs,
- Oyster Dishes,
- Pudding Pans,
- Patty Pans,
- Pie Pans,
- Pond Lily Shades,
- Refrigerators,
- Syrup Bottles,
- Star Individual Salts,
- Spice Boxes,
- Soup Ladles,
- School Sets,
- Shades and Holders,
- Study Lamps,
- Scoops,
- Stove Polish,
- Sapolio,
- Slipper Pockets,
- Sealing Wax,
- Tea Spoons,
- Table Spoons,
- Table Mats,
- Toilet Ware,
- Thermometers,
- Towel Racks,
- Teapots,
- Tea Trays,
- Tumbler Drainers,
- Vases,
- Wall Protectors,
- Whisk Brooms,
- Wicks,
- Wire Dish Covers,
- Water Pails,
- Water Sets.

BIGGS HOUSE,

Prendergast & Jennings,

PROPRIETORS,

PORTSMOUTH, OHIO.

MASSIE HOUSE,

PRENDERGAST & JENNINGS,

PROPRIETORS,

Portsmouth, Ohio.

R. BRUNNER,

Dealer in

DRY GOODS, CARPETS,

OIL CLOTHS, MATTINGS, RUGS, WINDOW SHADES, ETC.

Cor. 2d and Market Sts., Portsmouth, Ohio.

WHOLESALE DRY GOODS,

ESTABLISHED TWENTY-ONE YEARS.

J. F. TOWELL,

WHOLESALE DEALERS IN

DRY GOODS AND NOTIONS,

129 FRONT STREET, PORTSMOUTH, OHIO.

I am constantly supplied with a magnificent stock of

FOREIGN AND DOMESTIC DRY GOODS,

Suitable to the Seasons, and which I propose to sell as heretofore, in competition with any market.

On the first, second and third floors of my building will be found the choicest styles of the choicest goods. Discarding all trashy goods, and purchasing only those of the latest and freshest designs, my stock will please merchants of taste and judgment. My stock embraces in part:

Brown and Bleached Sheetings and Shirtings, Ticks,
 Prints, Ginghams, Delaines, Merinoes, Alpacas, Poplins,

Cloths, Cassimeres, Tweeds, Jeans, Satinets, Drills,
 Flannels, White Goods, Hosiery, Gloves, Fancy Baskets

Fancy Soaps, and all kinds of small wares pertaining to a first-class Notion House.

Maysville and Zanesville Cotton Yarns, Batting and Carpet Chain.

I would invite the merchants of Southern Ohio, Eastern Kentucky, and Western Virginia to visit my house.

Goods will be shown cheerfully, or price lists will be furnished by mail, when desired.

Traveling Agents: P. J. Reed, G. W. Betts, Geo. Scott.

J. F. TOWELL.

Mrs. Nickells & Co.,
Portsmouth, Ohio,
Dealers in
Millinery, Ribbons, Flowers and Feathers,
Hats and Bonnets,
In all the new shapes.

N. Side 2d St., bet. Market & Court, PORTSMOUTH, O.

V. REINHART & CO.,
—WHOLESALE—
CONFECTIONERS,
And Dealer in
Foreign & Canned Fruits, Nuts, Fireworks, etc.

Market Street, PORTSMOUTH, O.

H. H. BUSKIRK,
Dealer in
Staple and Fancy Groceries,
Portsmouth, O.

DAMARIN & CO.,

Wholesale Dealers in

Staple and Fancy Groceries.

GEO. W. WATKINS,

Sign of the Big Book, Second Street,

PORTSMOUTH, OHIO,

Dealer in

Books & Stationery.

ECLIPSE LIVERY STABLE.

T. M. LYNN - - Proprietor.

Second Street, West of Market, Portsmouth, O.

Livery Teams of all kinds furnished in the Finest Style.

H. P. PURSELL,

Dealer in

Drugs, Medicines, Chemicals, Perfumery, Toilet and Fancy Articles.

Cigars and Baking Powder *A SPECIALTY.*

Every Lady Should Use our Opera House Baking Powder.

Opera House Drug Store,
Cor. 4th and Court Sts., Portsmouth, O.

Miss M. LLOYD,

Millinery and Fancy Goods,

S. W. Corner Chillicothe and 4th Sts.

Farmers' National Bank,

PORTSMOUTH, OHIO,

Capital Paid in - - $250,000.

☞ Particular attention paid to collections, and proceeds promptly remitted.

New York Correspondent:
Ninth National Bank.

GEO. DAVIS, President. *J. M WALL*, Cashier.

Misses COE & KEER,

MILLINERS,

2d St., Portsmouth, O.

W. W. LITTLE.   ED. N. HOPE.

W. W. LITTLE & CO.,

Wholesale and retail dealers in

ASHLAND, POMEROY, PITTSBURG and ANTHRACITE COAL,

Have facilities for filling orders for any quantity on short notice.

Steamboats supplied with Coal at Wharf, all hours, Day or Night.

OFFICE—Corner Front and Court Streets.

MRS. TROTTER,
FRENCH MILLINERY ESTABLISHMENT.

PATTERN BONNETS FOR THE TRADE.

North Side Second Street,
Between Court and Washington,

PORTSMOUTH, OHIO.

GEORGE FISHER,
Druggist & Apothecary,

NORTHWEST CORNER OF

Chillicothe and Sixth Streets,

PORTSMOUTH, OHIO.

Keeps constantly on hand a full line of everything pertaining to

THE DRUG BUSINESS.

Prescriptions Carefully Prepared at all Hours.

WM. I. GRAY & CO.,

DEALERS IN

General Merchandise

Retailing at Wholesale Prices.

JOHN JONES,
PLUMBING, GAS, AND STEAM FITTING,
PLUMBERS' GOODS, STEAM WHISTLES,

Pumps, Steam and Water Gauges, Globe and Check Valves, Gas, Steam and Water Cocks,

Second Street, between **Market and Court.**
PORTSMOUTH, OHIO.

FISHER & CO.,
Grocers, Bakers and Confectioners.

Second Street, beween Court and Washington.

JOHN WILHELM,
Grocer and Produce Dealer,

Wilhelm's Opera House,

PORTSMOUTH, OHIO.

C. P. DENNIS,	WILHELM & CONROY,
DENTIST,	Manufacturers of
	TIN, COPPER
	—— AND ——
	Sheet Iron Ware,
OFFICE:	And dealers in Stoves, Grates and
Cor. of Second and Washington Streets.	Hollow-Ware,
	Second Street, near Court,
Portsmouth, Ohio.	PORTSMOUTH, OHIO.

W. H. JOHNSON & CO.,

121 Second Street,

PORTSMOUTH, O.,

Wholesale and Retail Dealers in

DRY GOODS

AND

CARPETS,

Invite the attention of the public to

FIRST-CLASS GOODS,

—SOLD AT—

Uniform Prices!

W. H. JOHNSON & CO.

Valley Book Store,

MARKET STREET, PORTSMOUTH, OHIO.

JOBBERS AND RETAILERS OF

School, Miscellaneous & Blank Books

WRITING PAPERS, ENVELOPES, STATIONERY,

Wall Papers, Window Shades and Cornices,

Pictures, Frames, Gilt Mouldings and Fancy Goods.

Give us a Call.

J. F. DAVIS,	D. L. JONES,
formerly of Davis, Threlkeld & Co., Cin.	of Ricker & Jones.

DAVIS & JONES,

Wholesale and Retail

DRUGGISTS,

123 West Front Street,

Portsmouth, O.

[12]

A. SEEL,

BAKERY, CONFECTIONERY,

—AND—

ICE CREAM SALOON.

PARTIES SUPPLIED,

No. 11 West Second Street.

JOS. G. REED.   JOHN PEEBLES.

REED & PEEBLES,

WHOLESALE DEALERS IN

Notions, Hosiery, White Goods

—AND—

SPECIALTIES IN DRY GOODS,

Market Street, West Side, near Front.

Portsmouth, O.

THOS. T. YEAGER.   JOHN DICE.

City Livery and Sale Stables

YEAGER & DICE, Proprietors,

MARKET STREET, BETWEEN THIRD AND FOURTH,

PORTSMOUTH, OHIO.

Horses kept by the Day or Week. Terms Reasonable.

ADVERTISEMENTS. 171

SAM'L M'CONNELL,   T. J. PURSELL,   H. A. TOWNE.
M. D. WILLIAMS,   E. B. GREENE,   R. A. MITCHELL.

Scioto Star Fire Brick Works

McConnell, Towne & Co.,

Manufacturers of

Scioto Fire Brick

OF ANY DESIRED SIZE AND SHAPE,

Inwalls, Bosh and Hearth Brick for Furnaces, and every variety of Tiles for Stoves, Grates, Boilers, Gas and Coal Oil Works, &c., &c.

Also, Fine Ground Fire Clay.

Prompt Attention Given to Orders.

(Address,)   PORTSMOUTH, OHIO.

FANCY PASTRY FLOUR,

"Limestone Mills,"

—BY THE—

Barrel, Half-Barrel and Sack.

M. W. THOMPSON & SON,

134 West Second Street,

PORTSMOUTH, O.

Lehman, Richman & Co.,

MANUFACTURERS OF

CLOTHING

—AND—

Jobbers in Woolens,

127 Front Street, Portsmouth, O.

ENOS REED,
DRUGGIST,

Tribune Building, Cor. 2nd and Court Sts.,

Portsmouth, Ohio.

Specialties:

**Pure Flavoring Extracts,
Lemon, Vanilla, Strawberry,
Pine Apple, Celery and Rose.**

Pure Ground Pepper, Cinnamon, Cloves, Allspice,

Cream Tartar and Soda.

L. R. MORGAN,
Successor to Flanders & Morgan,

MERCHANT TAILOR, CLOTHIER,
———— AND DEALER IN ————

Gents' Furnishing Goods, Trunks,
Childrens' Suits, Etc.

Massie Block, Market Street, Portsmouth, Ohio.

TO HOUSEKEEPERS.

When Baking Powder is to be used in any of the Recipes of this Book, be sure and buy

Maguire's Unrivaled Baking Powder,
Manufactured only by
A. D. MILLER, Proprietor,
PORTSMOUTH, OHIO.

It is pronounced by those who use it the best manufactured. Ask your grocer for it.

Also proprietor of Miller's Diarrhœa Mixture and Cough Honey, the safest remedies offered. No family should be without them.

ADVERTISEMENTS. 173

Insurance Agency.

W. H. BONSALL.   DAN. M'FARLAND, JR.

W. H. BONSALL & CO.,
118 West Second Street.

Losses of this agency at Portsmouth, paid within the last 6 years, to July 1, '73.

Fire............$37,169 00	**Prompt attention given to all matters pertaining to Insurance.**
Hull............10,250 00	
Life............10,000 00	
Accident........3,052 00	
Cargo...........2,171 00	

JOHN YOAKLEY,
Dealer in
Pianos, Organs and Violins,
All Kinds of Strings,
Musical Instruments, Musical Merchandise,
And Sheet Music.
118 West Second Street, Portsmouth, Ohio.

General agent for Pianos and Organs of every make—Special agent for none.

B. AUGUSTIN,
Manufacturer and dealer in
AMERICAN AND FRENCH CANDIES,
Fruits and Nuts of all kinds, etc.,
Second Street, near Market.

Pianos and Organs.

DECKER BROS. UNRIVALED PIANOS,
The Favorite Valley Gem Pianos,
Estey's Cottage Organs,

And a great variety of other Pianos and Organs for sale or to rent until paid for.
D. S. JOHNSTON,
Washington Street, bet. 3d and 4th, Portsmouth, Ohio.

J. W. MARCH.   DAVID OVERMAN,
of Hillsboro, O.

J. W. MARCH & CO.,
WHOLESALE DEALERS IN

Boots, Shoes, Hats, Caps, &c.

Market Street,
PORTSMOUTH, OHIO.

CH. C. BODE,
Freestone and Marble Works
GALLIA STREET, BETWEEN GAY AND BOND,
Portsmouth, Ohio.
Post Office Box 178.

All Orders Promptly Attended to, and Satisfaction Guaranteed.

I. REITZ.   CH. C. BODE.

REITZ & BODE,
Contractors and Builders,
—— AND DEALERS IN ——
SAWED & BLOCK STONE,

ORDERS FILLED ON SHORT NOTICE.

MISS EMMA BELL,
—— DEALER IN ——
Children's Wear, Mourning Goods,
TOILET ARTICLES, &c.,
Stamping Done to Order in New Patterns.
Second Street, between Court and Washington,
PORTSMOUTH, OHIO.

H. EBERHARDT & CO.,
Dealers in
STOVES, TINWARE, MANTLES, ETC., ETC.,

The Celebrated **ANDES** COOK STOVE, Coal and Wood

Market Street, West Side, Between Front and Second,
PORTSMOUTH, O.

SCIOTO HAT COMPANY,
— DEALERS IN —
Hats, Caps, Furs,
Gents' Furnishing Goods, &c.
605 Chillicothe Street,
Three doors North of Sixth Street.

W. E. HANCOCK,

Fruit, Fish and Oyster

DEALER,

NO. 106 SECOND STREET,

Portsmouth, O.

M. F. Micklethwait & Bro.,

DEALERS IN

Family Groceries,

CORNER OF

Market and Second Streets,

PORTSMOUTH, OHIO.

Scioto Valley Fire Brick Co.,

MANUFACTURERS OF

WILSON'S IMPROVED
CALCINED FIRE BRICK,

OF EVERY SIZE AND SHAPE,

IN-WALLS, BOSH AND HEARTH BRICK FOR FURNACES,

——AND EVERY VARIETY OF——

Tiles for Stoves, Grates, Boilers, Gas and Coal Oil Works.
ALSO, FINE GROUND FIRE CLAY.

JOHN DICE,

——MANUFACTURER OF——

CARRIAGES,

Buggies and Light Wagons,

SECOND STREET,

PORTSMOUTH, OHIO.

A. LORBERG,

MERCHANT TAILOR

AND DEALER IN

Gents' Furnishing Goods,

109 West Second Street,

PORTSMOUTH, OHIO.

GEORGE DAVIS & CO.

Manufacturers and Dealers in

Flour, Feed, Lime, Cement, Etc.,

Second Street, between Market and Court.

M. F. TIMMONDS.   S. D. TIMMONDS.

M. & S. Timmonds

Wholesale and Retail Dealers in

Groceries and Produce,

Crackers, Bread and Boat Stores,

FRONT STREET, OPPOSITE WHARFBOAT,

Portsmouth, O.

Planing Mill and Lumber Yard.

H. LEET & CO.

——DEALERS IN——

Pine and Domestic Lumber,

Shingles, Pine and Poplar Flooring.

Will Furnish Doors, Sash and Blinds on Short Notice.

Corner of Ninth and Washington Streets.

R. M. LLOYD,

Extensive Retail Dealer at

WHOLESALE PRICES

———(IN)———

BOOTS and SHOES

Keeps the largest stock in the city, and sells at

EXTREMELY LOW FIGURES

603 Chillicothe Street,

TWO DOORS NORTH OF SIXTH,

PORTSMOUTH, O.

PARK DRUG STORE,

M. S. PIXLEY, - Proprietor.

Pure Drugs and Patent Medicines,

A SPECIALTY.

Brushes, Combs, Perfumery,

And Fine Toilet Articles,

Of the best manufacture, well selected.

PRESCRIPTIONS CAREFULLY COMPOUNDED.

ST. JAMES HOTEL,

4th St., Cincinnati, O.

J. J. McGRATH - - - Proprietor.

Remodeled, Refurnished, Enlarged,

1874!

E. B. LODWICK.   A. H. STEIN.   C. S. GREEN.

Walnut Street House,

East Side of Walnut St., bet. 6th and 7th Sts.,

CINCINNATI, OHIO.

LODWICK, STEIN & CO. - - Proprietors.

Having just taken possession of this old established House, the Proprietors have made thorough repairs and general improvements. Good rooms and well furnished will be provided their guests, and a table unsurpassed in the city.

We extend a special invitation to our Portsmouth and up-river friends, and invite them to stop with us.

CRAWFORD HOUSE,

Corner of Sixth and Walnut Streets,

CINCINNATI, OHIO.

I Pride myself in providing for my guests the

BEST LIVING, CLEANEST HOUSE,

And

More Civility

For Less Money than any other House in the City.

COME AND SEE ME!

FRANK J. OAKES,

Proprietor.

CONTENTS.

SOUP. PAGE.

General Directions...Corn...Potato... Beef...Oyster...Okra . Vegetable ...Rice...Macaroni...White...Turkey...Mutton...Bean...Brunswick... 9...13

FISH.

General Directions...Boiled Sea Fish... Fried Shad...Mackerel...Halibut...Cod Fish...Fried Fish....Pickled Salmon...Fried Bass...Boiled... Broiled Shad, Fresh...Boiled Shad, Salt...Fried Cat Fish...Salt Cod Fish...Fried Frogs... 13...16

SAUCES FOR FISH.

For Tripe, Herring and Lobsters...Drawn Butter...Egg................. 17

OYSTERS.

Pie...Escaloped...Pickled...Fried 2 .... 18...19

MEATS.

General Directions...Head Cheese...Boiled Ham...Fried Ham and Eggs...Sausages...Lard...Pork and Beans...Cold Beef...Dried Beef... Corn Beef....Beef Tongue Salad...Spiced Beef...Steak...Meat Cakes... Fried Liver...Roasted Lamb...Lamb Chops...Broiled Lamb Steak... Lamb Cutlets...Boiled Leg of Mutton...Veal Loaf 2...Veal Pie... Cream Omelet...Delicate Omelet...Omelet...Ham Omelet...Buttered Eggs...Poached Eggs...Stuffed Eggs...Boiled Eggs...Fried Eggs.. 20...29

SAUCE.

Onion...Tomato...Celery...Mustard.. 29...30

POULTRY AND GAME.

General Directions...Boiled Chicken Pot Pie...Chicken Pie...Pie Crust...Roast Duck or Goose...Roast Turkey 2...Prepared Turkey for Cooking...Roast Pheasant...Roast Quail...Jellied Chicken...Roast Fowl...Roast Partridge .... 30...33

CHICKEN SALAD.

Chicken Salad 5... 34...35

VEGETABLES.

General Directions...Baked Egg Plant...Fried Egg Plant...Salsify Dressed as Oysters...Young Onions Stewed...Parsnips...Asparagus...Stewed Onions...Macaroni...Cold slaw 3...Cabbage Salad...Delicious Slaw...Fried Rice...Preserving Corn...Fried Corn...Baked Tomatoes 2...Fried Tomatoes...Canned Tomatoes and Corn...Baked Corn...Stewed Corn...Green Corn Pudding...Corn Oysters...Corn Pudding...Browned Potatoes with Meat...Mashed Potatoes 2...Green Peas 3...Baked Potatoes...Cooked Beans...Saratoga Potatoes...Fried Potatoes 2... 35...43

YEAST.

Rising...Yeast 3... 44

BREAD.

Bread...Rolls...Soft Raised Rolls...Tea Cake...Milk Toast...Pocket Books...Milk Rising Bread...New England Mixed Bread...Bread Gems...Rusk...To Make Bread...Hot Cross Buns........................ 45...48

BISCUITS.

Baking Powder...Mush...Short...Bath...Maryland...Short Cake for Fruit...Soda...Tea .... 48...49

CORN BATTER CAKES.

Corn Johnny Cake...Rice Pone...Batter Cakes...Johnny Cakes...Corn Bread 3...Virginia Corn Bread...Sweet Corn Bread........................ 50...51

BROWN BREAD.

Rye...Boston Brown...Brown 2...Boston...Graham 2...Brown Bread Cakes...Steamed Boston Bread .... 52...53

MUFFINS, ETC.

Sally Lunn...German Puffs 2...Pop-Overs...Puffets...Snow Flakes...Sutherland Muffins...Muffins 4...Rye or Graham Muffins............... 54...55

FRITTERS.

Batter Cakes...Waffles...Bread Pan Cakes...Fritters...Alice's Waffles... 56...57

PIES.

Pastry...Minced Meat...Mince...Mock Mince...Temperance Mince... Pumpkin 2...Flour...Peach Cobblers...Custard...Cheese Cake...Sand Tarts...Dedham Cream...Puff Paste...Pie-Plant...Cocoanut...Kentucky...Pastry...Lemon 6...Lemon Puffs...Lemon Cheese Cake... Cream Pies 3... 57...64

PUDDINGS.

Tapioca 2...Lemon Sauce...Soufle—Cottage...Orange...Taylor...Pudding...Jelly...Snow...Citron...Sunderland...Huntington...Custard... Corn Starch...Suet...Lemon Butter...Plum...Revere House...Dandy ...Fig...Delmonico...Sweet Potato...Kiss...Sauce for Pudding 2... Pudding...Dried Cherry...Plum...Bread Plum...Queen's Bread... Transparent...Baked Indian 2...Bread and Butter...Suet...Cracker.... Starch...Steam...Apple...Cream Batter...Poor Man's 2...Apple Dumplings...Cracker Dessert...Apple, Currant or Damson...Cocoanut Custard...Tapioca Custard...Baked Custard 2...Chocolate Cream Custard...Apple Custard...Flummery...Cocoanut Blanc Mange... Charlotte Russe 2...Apple Float 2...Float.................. 65...78

SAUCE FOR PUDDINGS.

Cream...Cold...Elegant Pudding........................... 79

CUSTARDS, CREAMS, ETC.

Whipped Cream...Gelatine...Lemon Cream...Raspberry Cream... Spanish Cream..Ice Cream...Philadelphia Ice Cream...Bavarian Cream...Italian Cream 2...Spanish Cream...Cream Charlotte... Lemon Jelly...Cocoanut Cream...Pie Plant Jelly...Quince Jelly... Crab Apple Jelly...Spiced Peaches...Spiced Tomatoes...Spiced Currants...Cranberry Sauce...Apple Sauce...Ambrosia...Sugared Oranges...Stewed Pears...Stewed Prunes...Apple Butter...Tomato Butter...Stewed Apples, whole...Orange Marmalade...Currant, Strawberry or Raspberry Jam...Apple Butter...Quince Butter... Raspberry Jam...Tomato Honey................................ 80...87

PRESERVES.

General Directions...Peach...Tomatoes...Watermelon...Pears...Citron ...Orange and Lemon...Cherries...Strawberries................ 88...90

PICKLES.

Yellow...Damson...Peach...Pickles...Piccalilli...Pickled Currants...Martino...Plums 2...Green Tomato...Onion...Cucumber...Spanish...Green Walnut...Green...Stuffing for Mangoes............ 91...96

CHOW--CHOW.

Chow-Chow 3.. 96...97

PEPPER SAUCE.

Pepper Vinegar...Pepper Sauce...................................... 97

CATSUP.

Tomatoes 4...Cucumber...Gooseberry...Chilton Sauce...Walnut.......... 98...100

COFFEE, CHOCOLATE AND TEA.

Tea...Brown Coffee...Coffee...Chocolate........................ 100...101

CAKES.

General Directions...Citron 2...Fruit 7...Black...White Fruit...Measure Black...Black Fruit...Pound...Delicate 3...French Loaf 2...Cocoanut 6...Boiled Sponge...White Sponge...Berwick Sponge...Sponge 2...Ice Water Sponge...White Sponge...Old Virginia Sponge...White Mountain 2...Orange...Starch 2...Plain Mountain...Corn Starch...Cup 3...Lemon Jelly 4...Lemon Cake...Lemon Jelly for Cake...Silver...White 2...Yellow...Gold...Spice 3...Almond 2...Chocolate 3...Cream 2...Custard...Ginger Bread...Corn Bread...Soft Ginger Bread...Soft Ginger Cake 2...Mark Ginger Cake...Doughnuts 2...Crullers 2...Jumbles...Quaker...Cookies 2...Molasses Cookies... 101...118

MISCELLANEOUS CAKES.

Marble...Vanilla...Almond Macaroons...Marble...Bread...Split...Nut...Velvet...Thanksgiving...Jumbles...Ginger Snaps 3...Webster...Cocoanut Drops...Hickory Nut 2...Blackberry...Madison...Coffee...Delicious...Kisses...Queen's...Currant Loaf...Dried Apple...Lincoln...Clay...Federal...Munn...Clove...A Good Suggestion.............. 119...124

CANDY.

Butter Scotch 2...Chocolate Caramels 3...Sugar...Walnut...Home Made Cream...Cocoanut Drops...Everton Taffy............................ 125...127

REMEDIES AND FOOD FOR THE SICK.

General Remarks...To Cure Ague...For Cough...Lock-jaw...Boils...Night Sweats...Bowel Complaints...For Sore Breast 2...Cough Syrup...Cure for Cough...Cough Mixture...Cure for Dropsy...A Cold ...Remedy for Croup...Diarrhœa...Cure for Headache...Dried Flour for Feeding Children...Tea Leaves for Burns...Cure for Neuralgia...Sure Cure for Felon...Herb Teas...Corn Meal Gruel...Beef Tea...Toast Water...Vinegar Whey...Mulled Egg...Cream Nectar...Chicken Broth...Raspberry Shrub...Drink for Sick...Rice Jelly...Blackberry Cordial...Sago Gruel...Oyster Toast...Beef Tea...Corn Meal Gruel...Egg and Milk...Oat Meal Gruel...Pap of Boiled Flour...Sherbet...Smith's Cough Powder...Cure for Felon...Plaster for Gathered Breast...To Avoid a Cold...Anti-Cholera Mixture...For Frozen Flesh...Potato Poultice...Cure for Dyspepsia...For Corns...To Prevent Wounds from Mortifying...Cure for Wasp Stings...Hop Poultice...Mustard Plaster...Salve...To Cure a Wen...To Cure Diptheria...To Prevent Flies Injuring Picture Frames...To Cure White Swelling on the Knee...To Prevent a Felon...Simple Remedy for Rheumatism...Cure for Strain...Rock Candy Cough Mixture...A Speedy Remedy for Croup...Toothache Remedy...A Cure for Phthisic and Asthma...Cure for Scurvy or Canker Sore Mouth...Cure for Hoarseness..125...139

MISCELLANEOUS.

Hard Soap...Excellent Hair Wash...To take out Grease...A Cleaning Polish for Furniture...To Restore Gilt Frames...Cold Water Soap...To Clean Silver...For Disobedient Children...To Destroy Flies..To Clean Carpets 2...Washing Fluid...Death to Insects...To Remove Water Stains from Black Crape...Death to Bedbugs...To set the colors of Calicoes...Camphor Ice...To Clean White Paint....To Clean Brass Stair Rods....To Remove Pimples....Soft Soap...To Clean Straw Matting....Salve for Chapped Lips, etc....To Polish Furniture....To remove Odor......To remove Rust from Steel....To take Grease out of Silks...To Exterminate Roaches....Tooth Powder...Pearl Drops for the Skin ..To destroy Flies....Raspberry Vinegar 2....To Preserve Potatoes till Spring....To make an Old Fowl Tender....Fine Cologne Water....Lemon Ice....Ice (counterfeit pure) Cream....Cottage Cheese...How to Keep Meat....To Sweeten Casks....To Extinguish a Fire in a Chimney....To clean Mirrors....Scent Bags....To Purify Glass Vessels....Rose Hair Oil....Furniture Polish...Poisons, and their Antidotes..139...150

THE YOUNG LADY'S TOILETTE.................................150...151

www.ingramcontent.com/pod-product-compliance
Lightning Source LLC
Chambersburg PA
CBHW031830230426
43669CB00009B/1287